HANDY REFERENCE (1)

Keyboard Shortcuts

Moving

Cursor keys	Up/down/left/right one space
Ctrl + left/right	Previous/next word
Ctrl + up/down	Previous/next paragraph
Home/End	Beginning/end of line
Ctrl + Home/End	Beginning/end of document
PgUp/PgDn	Move up/down one screen
Ctrl + PgUp/PgDn	Move to top/bottom of window
Alt+Shift+Up/Down ...	Select paragraph and move up/down

Editing

Ctrl+NumPad5	Select entire document
Alt+Shift+NumPad5 .. (Numlock off)	Apply normal style
Return	New paragraph
Shift+Return	New line within paragraph
Ctrl+Return	New page
Ctrl+Shift+Return	New column
Ctrl+Shift+*	Display invisible characters
Ctrl+Backspace	Delete word to left
Ctrl+Delete	Delete word to right
Ctrl+Shift+C	Copy format
Ctrl+Shift+V	Paste format

Quick Formatting

Ctrl+B	Bold
Ctrl+I	Italic
Ctrl+Shift+A	All caps

Ctrl+Shift+K	Small caps
Ctrl+U	Normal underline
Ctrl+Shift+D	Double underline
Ctrl+Shift+W	Word underline
Ctrl+Shift+P	Enter point size
Ctrl+Shift+F	Enter font
Ctrl+=	Subscript
Ctrl and + ...	Superscript
Ctrl+Shift+>	Increase size
Ctrl+Shift+<	Decrease size
Ctrl+]	Increase by 1 point
Ctrl+[......................	Decrease by 1 point
Ctrl+Shift+[..............	Kern together
Ctrl+Shift+]	Kern apart
Ctrl+Space	Reset format to current style
Ctrl+Shift+S	Select style
Ctrl+L	Left align
Ctrl+E	Centre align
Ctrl+R	Right align
Ctrl+J	Justify
Ctrl+M	Indent
Ctrl+Shift+M	Decrease indent
Ctrl+T	Hanging indent
Ctrl+Shift+T	Decrease hanging indent
Ctrl+1	Single line spacing
Ctrl+2	Double line spacing
Ctrl+5	1.5 line spacing
Ctrl+Shift+Q	Apply Symbol font

Menu Options

Ctrl+N	New
Ctrl+O	Open
Ctrl+W	Close
Ctrl+S	Save
Ctrl+P	Print
Ctrl+Z	Undo

HANDY REFERENCE (2)

Keyboard Shortcuts (contd)

Ctrl+Y	Redo
Ctrl+X	Cut
Ctrl+C	Copy
Ctrl+V	Paste
Ctrl+A	Select All
Ctrl+F	Find
Ctrl+H	Replace
Ctrl+G	Go To
Alt+Ctrl+N	Normal view
Alt+Ctrl+O	Outline
Alt+Ctrl+P	Page Layout
Alt+Shift+R	Headers/footers
Ctrl+D	Font dialog
Ctrl+K	AutoFormat

Function Keys

F1	Help
Shift+F1	Context-sensitive help
F2	Move selected text
Shift+F2	Copy selected text
Ctrl+F2	Print preview
F3	Glossary entry
Shift+F3	Change case
Ctrl+F3	Cut to spike
Ctrl+Shift+F3	Insert spike
F4	Repeat previous command
Shift+F4	Find/Go To again
Ctrl+F4	Close document window
Alt+F4	Exit
F5	Go To
Shift+F5	Go back
Ctrl+F5	Restore document window
Ctrl+Shift+F5	Bookmark
Alt+F5	Restore Word window
F6	Next pane

Shift+F6	Previous pane
Ctrl+F6	Next document window
Ctrl+Shift+F6	Previous document window
F7	Spelling
Shift+F7	Thesaurus
Ctrl+F7	Move document window
Ctrl+Shift+F7	Update links
F8	Extend selection
Shift+F8	Reduce selection
Ctrl+F8	Resize document window
Ctrl+Shift+F8	Select column
F9	Update field
Shift+F9	Display selected field on/off
Ctrl+F9	Insert field manually
Ctrl+Shift+F9	Unlink field
Alt+F9	Display all fields on/off
Alt+Shift+F9	Activate field
F10	Activate menu
F11	Next field
Shift+F11	Previous field
Ctrl+F11	Lock field
Ctrl+Shift+F11	Unlock field
F12	Save as
Shift+F12	Save
Ctrl+F12	Open
Ctrl+Shift+F12	Print

Special Characters

Ctrl+Shift+Space	Nonbreaking space
Ctrl+Hyphen	Optional hyphen
Ctrl+Shift+Hyphen	Nonbreaking hyphen
Ctrl+Tab	Insert Tab (into table)
Alt+0xxxx (on numeric keypad)	Insert ANSI character code xxxx

HANDY REFERENCE (3)

Tips for Good Document Design

- Try not to use too many fonts or text effects. Often good results can be gained from restricting yourself to two basic fonts, one for headings and one for body text.

- Allow yourself the use of white space. It is usually not necessary to completely fill the page, and space can be used as a very effective way of adding emphasis.

- Make sure that your text is always readable. More than 40 characters (or 10 words) to a line puts a strain on the human eye. Also too little space between lines can create a solid mass of text which is very tiring to read.

- Use styles as much as possible. This way you have the flexibility to make design alterations to, for example, all your headings in one simple manoeuvre at any time.

- Make sure your document has a clear structure. In particular, check that main headings are obviously more prominent than sub-headings.

- Check the available templates to see if there is a ready-made document which suits your purposes. If not, you may still be able to adapt an existing template in order to create your own.

- Feel free to experiment with dummy text and graphics in the early stages of your design. Try to form a clear idea of which settings to use for document margins, text columns and page structure right from the beginning of your work.

- Keep your design as simple and consistent as possible.

ABOUT THE SERIES

In easy steps series is developed for time-sensitive people who want results fast. It is designed for quick, easy and effortless learning.

By using the best authors in the field, and with our experience in writing computer training materials, this series is ideal for today's computer users. It explains the essentials simply, concisely and clearly - without the unnecessary verbal blurb. We strive to ensure that each book is technically superior, effective for easy learning and offers the best value.

Learn the essentials **in easy steps** - accept no substitutes!

Titles in the series include:

Title	Author	ISBN
Windows 95	Harshad Kotecha	1-874029-28-8
Microsoft Office	Stephen Copestake	1-874029-37-7
Internet UK	Andy Holyer	1-874029-31-8
CompuServe UK	John Clare	1-874029-33-4
CorelDRAW	Stephen Copestake	1-874029-32-6
PageMaker	Scott Basham	1-874029-35-0
Quicken UK	John Sumner	1-874029-30-X
Microsoft Works	Stephen Copestake	1-874029-41-5
Word	Scott Basham	1-874029-39-3
Excel	Pamela Roach	1-874029-40-7
Sage Sterling for Windows	Ralf Kirchmayr	1-874029-43-1
Sage Instant Accounting	Ralf Kirchmayr	1-874029-44-X
SmartSuite	Stephen Copestake	1-874029-42-3
HTML	Ralf Kirchmayr	1-874029-46-6
Netscape Navigator	Mary Lojkine	1-874029-47-4
PagePlus	Richard Hunt	1-874029-49-0
Publisher	Brian Austin	1-874029-56-3
Access	Stephen Copestake	1-874029-57-1

To order or for details on forthcoming titles ask your bookseller or contact Computer Step on 01926 817999.

WORD
in easy steps

Scott Basham

In easy steps is an imprint of Computer Step
5c Southfield Road, Southam
Warwickshire CV33 OJH England
☎01926 817999

First published 1996

Notice of Liability

Every effort has been made to ensure that this book contains accurate
and current information. However, Computer Step and the author
shall not be liable for any loss or damage suffered by readers as a
result of any information contained herein.

Trademarks

Microsoft and Windows are registered trademarks of Microsoft
Corporation. All other trademarks are acknowledged as belonging to
their respective companies.

For all sales and volume discounts please contact Computer Step on
Tel: 01926 817999.

For export orders and reprint/translation rights write to the address
above or Fax: (+44) 1926 817005.

Printed and bound in the United Kingdom

ISBN 1-874029-39-3

Contents

CHAPTER ONE

Getting to Know Word

This chapter gets you started with Word quickly. It shows you how to open Word, and make sense of its screen layout.

Covers

Introduction

Word-processing was one of the first popular applications for the modern personal computer. In the early days it provided little more than the ability to enter and change text on a computer monitor. As time went on software and hardware improved, and features such as spell-checking and various type effects were added. Also, the number of users increased.

Microsoft Word for Windows is widely acknowledged as a leader in its field, and is one of the best selling packages in any software category.

Let's face it, with Word we're talking about a *big* package. It has retained the position as market leader by stuffing itself full of useful features, taking it from word-processing into the realms of graphical and data-oriented documents. At first it may seem to contain a bewildering array of options and controls, but many are there to make life easier – providing quick access to the most commonly used features.

A big package inevitably comes with a depressingly big reference manual, which will describe each and every function in minute detail. This book is not intended to replace the manual; instead you should view it as a more graphical teaching guide. Wherever possible pictures and examples are used rather than pages of text to explain and demonstrate the concepts covered.

To gain maximum benefit from this book:

- Make sure that you are first familiar with the Windows operating environment (i.e. using a mouse, icons, menus, dialog boxes etc.).

- It is important to experiment using your own examples; like many things you will find that practice is the key to competence.

Starting Word

If You Are Using Windows 95
Use the Start button to access the Programs menu, and select the Microsoft Word icon.

Alternatively, if a shortcut has been set up, then you can activate Word from this icon:

Microsoft
Word

If You Are Using Windows 3.1
From the Windows 3.1 Program Manager, you can start Word by double-clicking directly on its icon.

If you double-click on a Word file (with a .DOC extension), your machine will load Word and then automatically open the file.

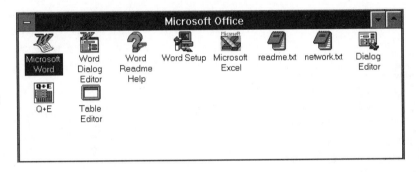

Alternatively, from the Windows 3.1 File Manager or Windows 95 Explorer locate the WINWORD.EXE file and double-click.

Tip of the Day
In Word Version 7, the "Tip of the Day" message normally appears as a toolbar at the top of the screen:

In Word 6, it appears as a dialog box. If you don't wish to see this, switch off the checkbox in the lower left corner.

The Word Screen

Title and Document Bar   Menus   Document Ruler

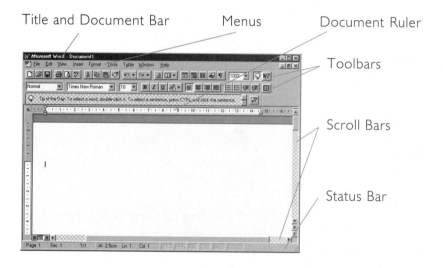

Toolbars

Scroll Bars

Status Bar

If you have just opened Word, you'll see something like this. Don't worry if there are extra items or things missing from this diagram; you'll see in a moment that it's possible to configure the Word screen in different ways.

A quick way to switch toolbars on and off is to hold down the right mouse button whilst within any currently visible toolbar.

Toolbars

Toolbars can appear at the top of the screen, at the bottom, or as floating palettes. They give you instant access to features without the need to search through menus and dialog boxes. There are eight toolbars in total, but we usually only require several at any time.

Activating/Deactivating Toolbars

Go to the View menu and choose Toolbars...

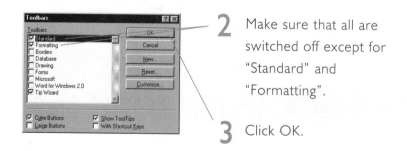

2 Make sure that all are switched off except for "Standard" and "Formatting".

3 Click OK.

Adjusting the Page Setup

Go to the File menu and choose "Page Setup". The Page Setup dialog box appears.

Click here if necessary to see the Margins settings.

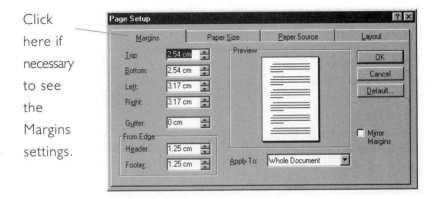

Tabbed Dialog Boxes

Many of Word's dialog boxes are *tabbed*, i.e. subdivided into sections. You can select your required section by clicking on the tab at the top of the box.

Click on the "Paper Size" tab

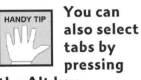

HANDY TIP

You can also select tabs by pressing the Alt key together with the underlined letter in the tab name. Alternatively, pressing Control together with the Tab key itself will cycle through each tab in turn.

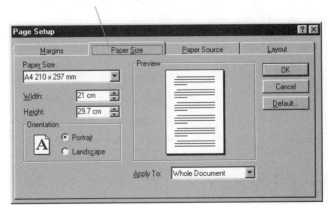

Help

If you press the F1 key while in a dialog box, then you'll see Help text about its options. Full on-line Help is available from the Help menu.

If you allow your mouse pointer to rest over an icon for a moment, a help box will appear. This gives you a brief explanation of the icon's function. In addition to this, the Status bar at the bottom of the screen will give a longer description.

help box

You can also access the on-line Help (from the Help menu), or use the Help icon at the top right of the screen. Click on this, then click on an icon or menu option to make the relevant help text appear.

Page Views

You can also use the View icons to switch between views:

There are four different ways of viewing the page, selectable from the top section of the View menu:

- **Normal**: Allows fast editing, previewing most (but not all) text effects.

- **Outline**: Views your text as a structured outline.

- **Page Layout**: Displays your document as actual pages, previewing text and graphics effects.

- **Master Document**: A special form of Outline view, used for long or structured documents.

Leaving Word

You can exit from Word in the normal way by choosing "Exit" from the File menu or by clicking on the Windows 95 Close box: ☒

(In Windows 3.1 double-click on the Control Menu: .)

CHAPTER TWO

Basic Text Manipulation

This chapter helps you start entering and manipulating text on the screen. It looks at different ways of editing and formatting type, as well as saving and printing your work.

Covers

The Document Window

 The New
Document icon

1 If there is no Document window, then create a new one by clicking on the "New" icon in the top left of the standard toolbar.

2 Enter a sentence of example text.

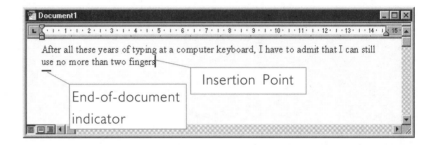

The vertical line is your Insertion Point, indicating where new text will appear. You can move the Insertion Point by:

- Using the cursor (arrow) keys.

- Clicking a new position with the mouse.

Word automatically works out when to take a new line without breaking words. If you want to start a new paragraph, press the Return or Enter key.

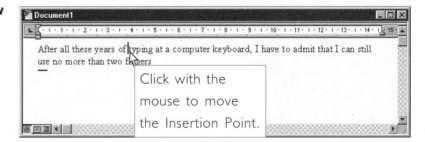

Inserting Text

Move the Insertion Point to a point where you would wish to add more text.

2 Type the text. It will appear at the Insertion Point.

Note that the words to the right of the Insertion Point move along to accommodate the new text:

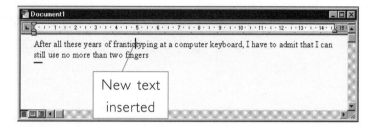

New text inserted

Deleting Text using Backspace

1 Move the Insertion Point so that it is directly after the text you want to delete.

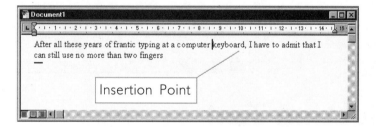

Insertion Point

2 Press the Backspace key once to erase each character to the left of the Insertion Point.

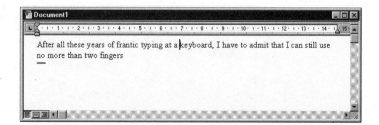

Deleting Text with the Delete Key

1 This time move the Insertion Point before the text to be deleted.

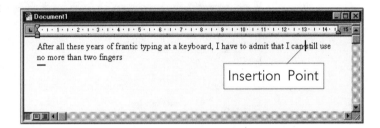

2 Press the Delete key once for each character to be deleted.

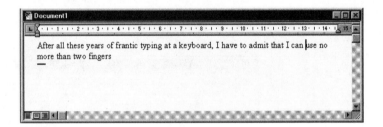

Selecting Text

You can select text by dragging horizontally across it using the mouse:

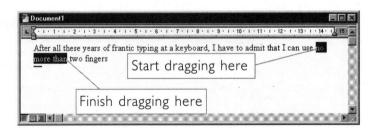

Replacing Selected Text

Anything you type will automatically replace any text which is currently selected:

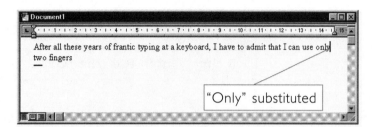

Adding More Text to the End of the Document

Remember that before adding more text to the end of your document, you must first reposition the Insertion Point:

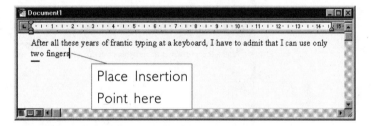

Note that, to start a new line at the end of the document, you must first click at the end of the last line.

2 Add the text:

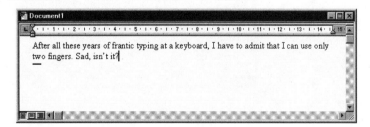

Insert versus Overtype

At the bottom of the screen, in the Status bar, the letters "OVR" should be greyed out. This indicates that you are in Insert, rather than Overtype mode.

1 Press the Insert key several times.

Each time you do this, the "OVR" indicator will select or deselect.

2 If necessary, press Insert again to activate Overtype mode.

In Overtype mode, new text overtypes (replaces) any text to the right of the Insertion Point.

3 Position the Insertion Point somewhere within your text:

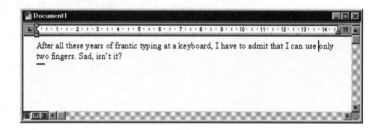

After all these years of frantic typing at a keyboard, I have to admit that I can use only two fingers. Sad, isn't it?

4 Type some new text.

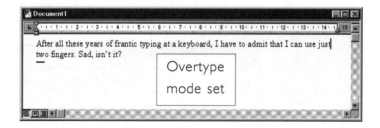

After all these years of frantic typing at a keyboard, I have to admit that I can use just two fingers. Sad, isn't it?

Overtype mode set

5 Use the Insert key to switch back to Insert mode.

Better Ways to Select Text

Choose the "Select All" option from the Edit Menu (or type Control + A).

Changing the Appearance of Text

Open the "Size" pop-up menu from the toolbar, and increase the point size of the text to twice the previous value.

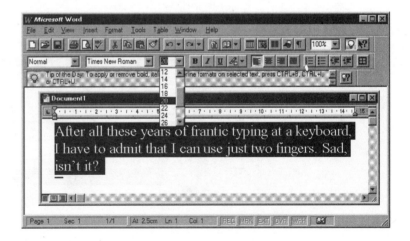

2 Select a single word and use the toolbar to switch on the Bold effect.

HANDY TIP

The keyboard shortcut for Bold is Control+Shift+B.

Click here to switch Bold on and off

3 If you want to select text over more than one line, either drag over the area required or click at one end of the selection, then hold down Shift and click at the other end:

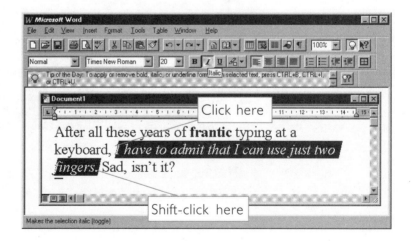

Click here

Shift-click here

4 You can also select whole lines of text by dragging vertically over the area within the left margin.

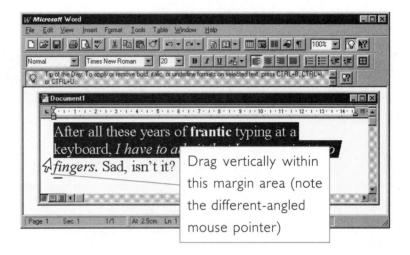

Drag vertically within this margin area (note the different-angled mouse pointer)

5 You can also double-click to select a single word, or triple-click to select an entire paragraph.

6 Note if you click an Insertion Point and then type more text, the new text takes its attributes (appearance) from the previous character.

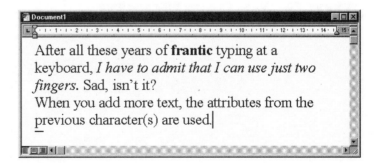

Saving a Document

The Save icon

To Save your work either choose "Save" from the File menu, or click on the Save icon in the toolbar.

The following dialog box will appear:

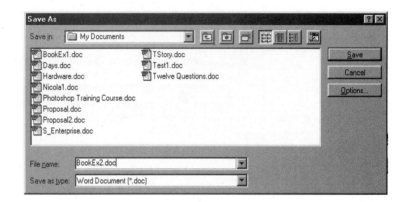

2 If necessary, select the correct drive and directory.

3 Enter the filename and click "Save".

4 If you have finished with the document, choose "Close" from the File menu.

Opening a Document

Either

- Choose "Open" from the File menu or click on the Open icon: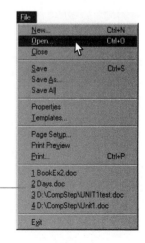

Or

- The last few files used are listed in the lower section of the File menu, and can be selected directly.

Printing a Document

| Either choose "Print" from the File menu, or click on the Print icon in the Toolbar: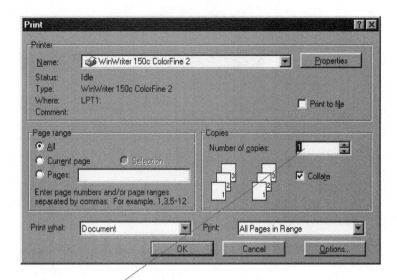

The following dialog box will appear:

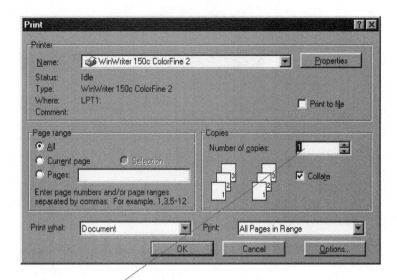

2 Enter the number of copies required.

3 Click "OK" to go ahead, or "Cancel" to abort.

Automatic Correction

Word 7 will normally highlight words not found in its dictionary. A red wavy line indicates a suspect word.

To deal with this:

1 Hold down the right mouse button to bring up a menu of spelling options.

HANDY TIP

To access the complete range of spelling options, choose "Spelling" from the pop-up menu, the Tools menu, the Spell icon in the toolbar or by pressing F7.

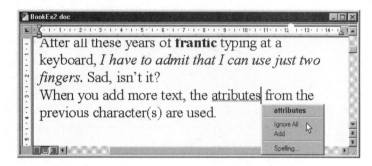

After all these years of **frantic** typing at a keyboard, *I have to admit that I can use just two fingers.* Sad, isn't it?
When you add more text, the atributes from the previous character(s) are used.

attributes

Ignore All
Add

Spelling...

This contains a list of the entries in the current dictionary which most closely match the underlined word.

BEWARE

Word will sometimes mistakenly correct where it shouldn't, e.g. changing "MSc" to "Msc". If this happens, choose "Undo" from the Edit menu. If you use Undo in this way with Word 7, it "learns" and will thereafter leave that particular word alone.

2 If the correct word is in the list, then select it to replace the incorrect version.

3 Choose "Ignore All" to ignore the word. You may wish to do this if the word is a proper noun, for example.

4 Choose "Add" to add the word to the current dictionary.

Intellisense

This is a feature which allows Word to make corrections as you type. An example of a common error is a word beginning with two capitals (e.g. "WEdnesday").

Word 7 Intellisense is more sophisticated, dealing with more errors. One example is the CAPS lock activated by mistake: it will correct "wEDNESDAY" to "Wednesday" then switch off the CAPS lock.

CHAPTER THREE

Character-level Formatting

This chapter starts looking at ways in which you can change the appearance of your text. All the effects discussed here apply on a character-by-character basis, as opposed to paragraph-level attributes, which are dealt with in the next chapter.

Covers

Introduction

What does "Character-level" mean?

Character-level attributes include font name, size, emboldening, underlining plus all sorts of other effects which can be applied to individual characters. If required, every single character could be given different attributes (although this would tend to make your document look a little like a ransom letter).

Using the Formatting Toolbar

1 Select the text which you want to format.

2 Choose the font required from the pop-up menu in the toolbar:

If you highlight a portion of text, the toolbar will indicate its current formatting options.

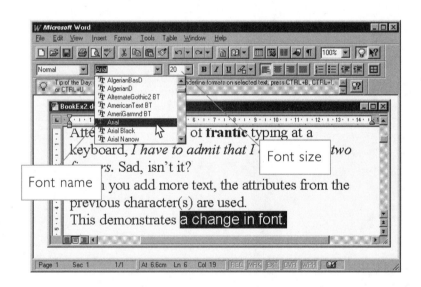

A font is a collection of characters with a particular visual style. Common fonts include:

Times or Times New Roman (useful for main text)
Arial (useful for headings)
Courier (the typewriter font)

3 Look at the font names in the pop-up list:

The most recently used fonts
appear above this line.

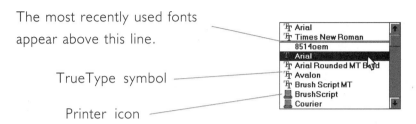

TrueType symbol

Printer icon

- A printer icon beside the name indicates a printer-font. Your machine will use the closest available screen font (which may not match the printed output exactly).

- A double T symbol indicates a TrueType font, which is used for both screen display and printing.

- No symbol beside the font name indicates a screen font. Always check that your printer can reproduce this to a high enough quality.

4 You can use the buttons on this toolbar to add effects such as Bold, Italic, and Underline:

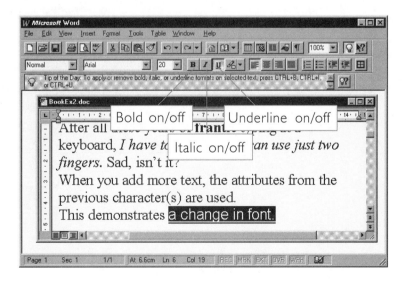

The Font Dialog Box

This controls all aspects of character-level formatting.

1 Select the text to change.

2 Either choose "Font" from the Format menu, or click your right mouse button inside the document window:

This brings up a pop-up menu containing options which are relevant to the task in hand. Later you will see that it changes depending on your current context.

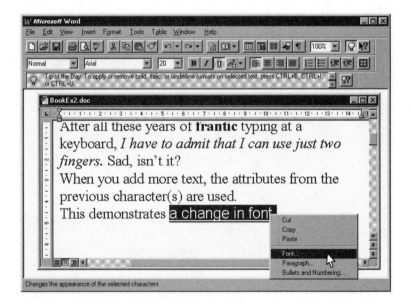

3 Choose "Font".

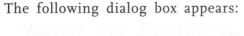

The following dialog box appears:

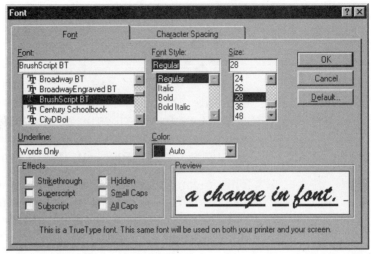

4   Experiment with the different options, noting how they affect the Preview image.

5   Click on the Character Spacing tab.

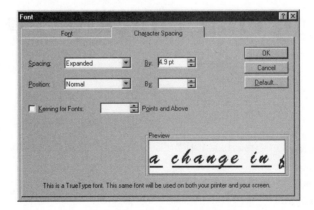

From here you can numerically control the character spacing, the position (for superscript and subscript), and kerning.

Kerning

Certain pairs of letters look odd with normal character spacing. Word uses kerning tables, which tell it how much closer together to bring them.

e.g. **To**
To

This process of examining each pair of adjacent characters in the document would slow down your machine considerably, so if you activate kerning you should set a threshold of approximately 12 points.

This means that Word will only consider text larger than 12 points for kerning. Spacing in small text is not so noticeable, so this will speed things up without a marked deterioration in quality.

To activate kerning:

1 Switch on the "Kerning for Fonts" checkbox.

2 Set the "Points and Above" value.

Changing Font Quickly

1 Select the text.

2 Press Control+Shift+F.

3 Type the first few letters of the font and press the Down Arrow key. You need to type enough letters to distinguish the font name from any others which may be similar.

4 Press Return.

HANDY TIP **Pressing Control+ Shift+F twice is another quick way of accessing the Font dialog box.**

CHAPTER FOUR

Paragraph-level Formatting

This chapter looks at ways of manipulating text on a paragraph-by-paragraph basis. It is often tempting to use the space bar to position text on the page, but this quickly leads to problems if text is edited or its attributes are changed. The benefits of alignment, indents and other automatic formatting features are well worth the time it takes to learn how to use these techniques.

Covers

Overview

What does "Paragraph-level" mean?

Options such as alignment, left and right indents, and space above and below refer to whole paragraphs, i.e. each paragraph has only one set of these attributes.

Formatting with the Toolbar

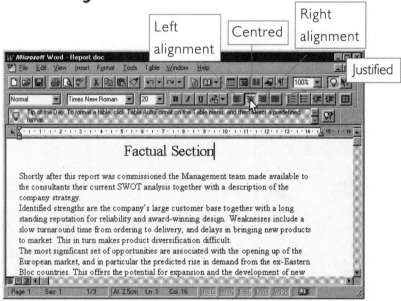

If you are changing just one paragraph you need only click an insertion point somewhere within it. Any change to a paragraph-level attribute will always affect the entire paragraph surrounding the Insertion Point.

1. Select the paragraph(s) to format. Remember that a heading is often a single-line paragraph.

2. Choose the form of alignment by clicking on the appropriate tool in the formatting toolbar.

Forms of Alignment

There are four forms of alignment:

Left
Text lines up along its left edge, with a ragged right edge.

Right
Here the text is moved so that the right edge is straight, and the left is ragged.

Centre
Text is centred between the left and right edges.

Justification
The text spacing is adjusted so that each line within a paragraph begins and ends in the same position (dictated by the margins and indents), giving a neat and regular appearance. Below is an example of justified text:

The last line of every justified paragraph is only aligned left, allowing the reader to easily distinguish one paragraph from another.

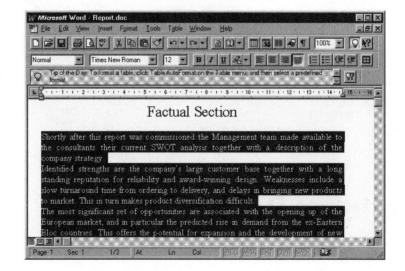

Numbered Paragraphs

1 Select the paragraphs to be numbered.

2 Click on the Numbering icon in the Formatting toolbar:

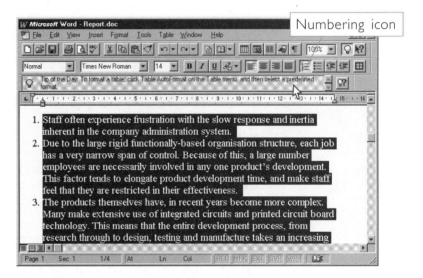

Removing Numbers

1 If necessary, re-select the numbered paragraphs.

2 Click on the Numbering icon a second time.

Bulleted Paragraphs

Activating Bullets

1 Select the paragraphs to be bulleted.

2 Click on the Bullet icon in the Formatting toolbar...

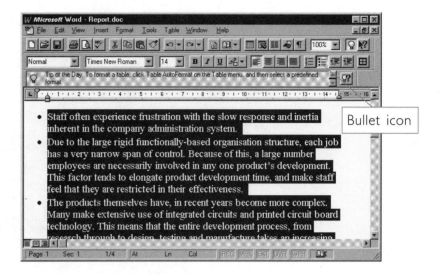

Bullet icon

Removing Bullets

1 If necessary, re-select the numbered paragraphs.

2 Click on the Bullet icon a second time.

The Paragraph Dialog Box

This controls all aspects of paragraph-level formatting.

1 Select the text to be formatted.

2 Either choose "Paragraph" from the Format menu, or click your right mouse button somewhere within the document window...

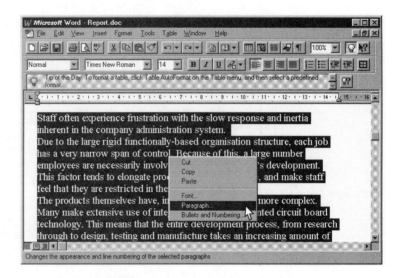

3 Select "Paragraph" from the pop-up menu.

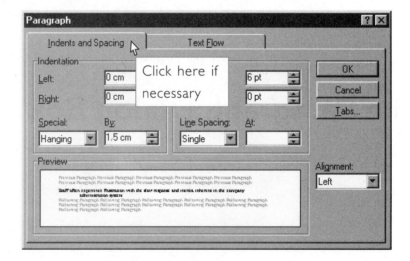

4 Experiment with the different paragraph controls, checking the results in the preview image.

You can adjust the left and right indent, the space above and below a paragraph, or the line spacing within a paragraph.

In the example below, a (vertical) "space before" of 6 points and a special hanging indent of 1.5cm have been set:

"Hanging indent" keeps the first line of each paragraph at the left margin, while moving all subsequent lines to the right by a fixed distance.

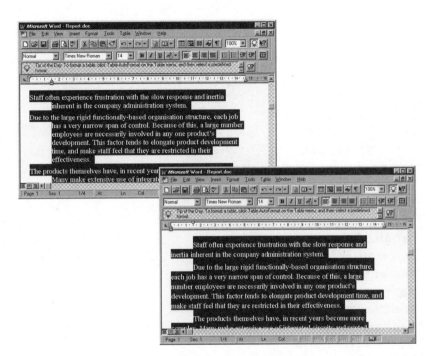

In the case above, a special first-line indent of 1.5cm has been set, and the line spacing has been changed to "exactly" 18 points. This means that each line in the selected paragraphs will be given exactly 18 points of vertical space regardless of the size of font.

The Points System of Measurement

This system was introduced firstly in the USA last century, and then adopted by the UK and some European countries.

72 points is equal to 1 inch. 12 points is equal to the size of normal typewriter text.

It provides a standard way of measuring the size of type, and often refers to the vertical dimension of characters in a given font. For this reason it is often useful to adjust vertical spacing using points, so that the space between paragraphs uses the same system as the paragraphs themselves.

...contd

The Text Flow Tab

1 Activate the Paragraph dialog box (either from the Format menu or by clicking in the document window with the right mouse button).

HANDY TIP **A widow is a single line of text at the beginning of a paragraph separated from the rest by a page break. An orphan is a similar line at the end of a paragraph. Both widows and orphans look unattractive and should be avoided if possible.**

2 Choose the Text Flow tab:

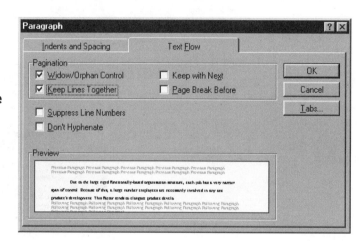

Widow/Orphan Control
This option instructs Word to automatically move text onto the next page if necessary to prevent widows and orphans occurring.

Keep Lines Together
Word will move the text so that the paragraph is not broken over two pages.

Keep With Next
Makes sure that the text is kept with the following paragraph, and not broken over two pages.

Page Break Before
Forces a new page at the start of the paragraph.

Suppress Line Numbers
Switches off numbering for this paragraph if line numbers have been used, renumbering the surrounding paragraphs if necessary.

Don't Hyphenate
Deactivates hyphenation.

CHAPTER FIVE

Working with a Document

This chapter helps you to find your way around a document, looking at scrolling, selecting different views and zooming in and out of the page. Additionally we'll look at Cut, Copy, Paste and the Format Painter tool.

Covers

Scrolling

When your text is too large for the document window, you'll need to use one of the following navigation methods:

Click here to scroll up

Scroll box

Click here to scroll down

Click here to scroll left

Scroll box

Click here to scroll to the right

The scroll boxes let you know where you are in a document. For example, when the vertical scroll box is right at the top of the scroll bar, you are looking at the top (the beginning) of the document.

As you scroll down, this box moves down like a lift through a lift shaft.

Quick Ways to Scroll

- Drag the scroll box directly to a new position.
- Click in the scroll bar to either side of the scroll box. The document will scroll in that direction one screen at a time.
- As you move your insertion point, Word will scroll automatically so that it can always be seen in the document window.

Zooming

You can use the Zoom pop-up menu to control the level of magnification used by the document window.

1 Either choose an option from the pop-up menu or enter a new percentage value between 10 and 200.

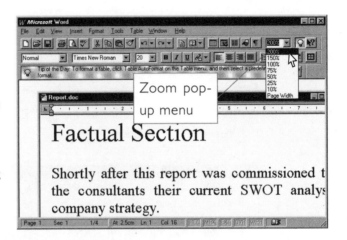

If you can afford the space on screen, always maximise both the document window and the Word window itself by clicking on the Maximise button in the top right corner of each.

2 The Page Width option automatically zooms in or out so that the entire width of the page is displayed.

3 In Page Layout view there are options to display one or more entire pages at a time.

Remember that the more you magnify the page, the more you'll need to scroll. Always try to view the entire horizontal line of text, since frequent horizontal scrolling can be tedious.

The Restore symbol indicates that a window is already maximised. Click on this to restore the window to its normal size.

Resizing Windows

The buttons used depend on your version of Windows:

	Windows 3.1	Windows 95
Maximise button	▲	☐
Restore button	⬍	⧉

The Ruler

The ruler gives you a visual account of the tabs and indents used for any selected text.

1   If the ruler is not visible, activate it by choosing "Ruler" from the View menu.

2   Select one or more paragraphs of text. Experiment by moving the indent markers:

First-line indent marker

General left indent marker

Default tab stops

Right indent marker

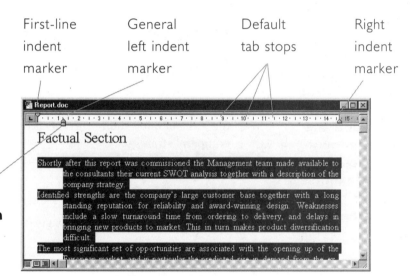

There is a small square block directly below the left indent marker. Dragging this will move both the left and first line indent markers together.

The Paragraph Dialog Box
You can also access these controls numerically from the Paragraph dialog box.

Normal and Page Layout View

You can select these either via the View menu, or by clicking on the View icons at the bottom left of the screen.

Normal View

This gives a preview of most text effects and some graphic effects. Screen redraw is fast, so this is the best view for most text editing.

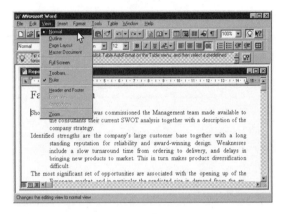

Page Layout View

This previews text and graphic effects, whilst still allowing full editing facilities.

Note the extra options in the Zoom pop-up menu.

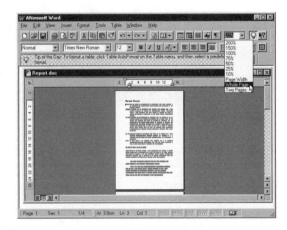

Cut and Paste

1 Select the text to be moved.

2 Holding down the right mouse button, choose "Cut".

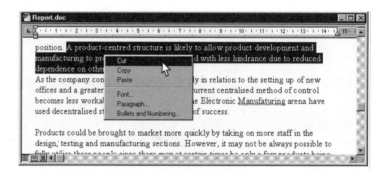

The text is removed and put into the Clipboard.

3 Next position the Insertion Point at the destination. Holding down the right mouse button, choose "Paste".

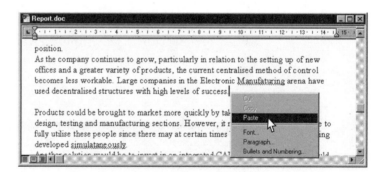

You can also Cut and Paste using the Edit menu, or the keyboard shortcuts Control+X, Control+V respectively.

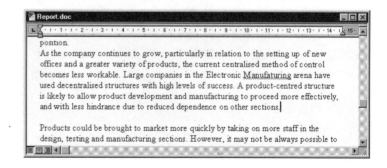

Copy and Paste

1 Select the text to be copied.

You can also Copy and Paste using the Edit menu, or the keyboard shortcuts Control +C, Control+V respectively.

2 Holding down the right mouse button, choose "Copy".

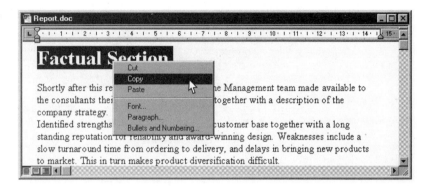

The quickest way to move text is to select it, then drag (from anywhere within the selected area) directly to the new position.

The text is copied into the Clipboard.

3 Next position the Insertion Point at the destination. Holding down the right mouse button, choose "Paste".

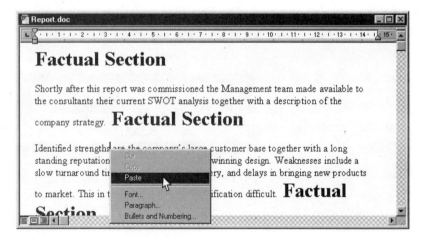

If you drag the selected area with the Control key held down, then the text will be copied to the new position.

Once something is in the Clipboard, you can paste it as many times as you like.

Undo and Redo

- Click the Undo button or type Control+Z to undo the last action.
- Alternatively, open the Undo pop-up menu to review and undo more than one action:

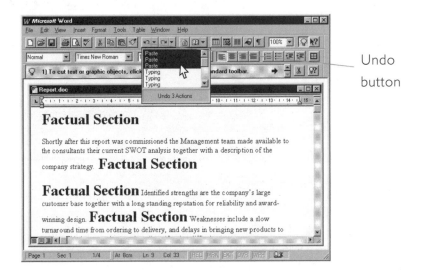

Undo button

- To redo the undone actions, type Control+Y or use the Redo pop-up menu.

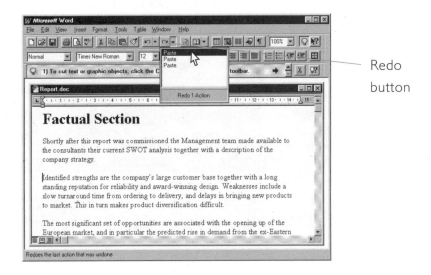

Redo button

Page Breaks

Word automatically calculates the position of page breaks. These appear in the document window as a dotted horizontal line (a "soft" page break).

1 To force a page break, choose "Break..." from the Insert menu.

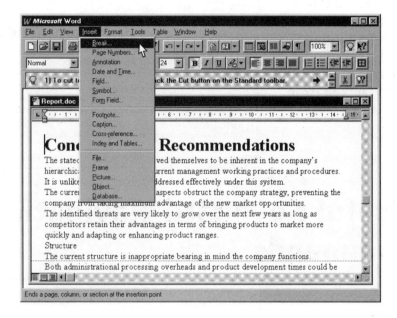

2 The following dialog box appears. Make sure that "Page Break" is selected and click "OK".

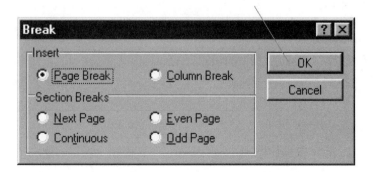

HANDY TIP The keyboard shortcut for page break is Control+ Return (or Enter). To delete a page break, simply select it by clicking in the left margin area and press Delete.

A "Hard" page break is inserted. The result appears as follows:

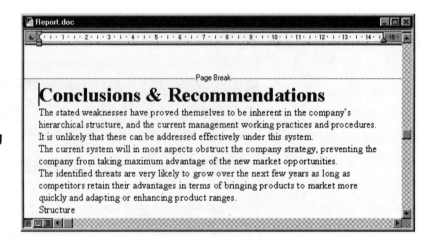

Useful Keyboard Navigation Commands

HANDY TIP If you hold down Shift while making a move, all the text between the old and the new position will be selected.

Cursor keys	Up/down/left/right one space
Control+left/right	Previous/next word
Control+up/down	Previous/next paragraph
Home/End	Beginning/end of line
Control+Home/End	Beginning/end of document
PgUp/PgDn	Move up/down one screen
Control+PgUp/PgDn	Move to top/bottom of window

The Format Painter

This allows you to copy the formatting options from one piece of text to another:

1 Select the source text and click on the Format Painter icon.

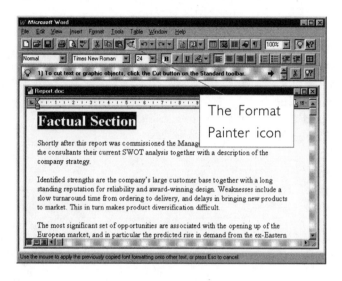

The Format Painter icon

HANDY TIP

To copy formatting to more than one destination, simply double-click the Format Painter icon. You can then apply the new formatting to as many pieces of text as you wish. When you've finished, either click back on the icon or press the Escape key.

2 Now drag across the destination text. The formatting is applied to the new text.

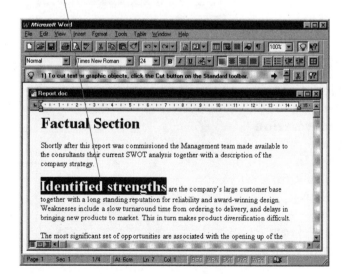

Document Properties

Windows 95 introduced file names which could be longer (and so more descriptive) than the Spartan eight characters allowed by MS-DOS. Even so, it is useful to record additional information as part of each Word document to help you organise your work, and remember your document's purpose.

Although there is no Properties option in Word 6, you can still access most of its features from "Summary Info" in the File Menu.

1 Go to the File menu and choose "Properties".

2 Enter the relevant details. These will be saved along with your document.

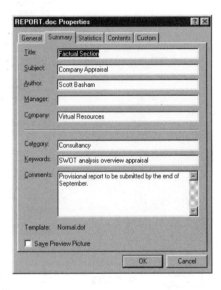

The Document Statistics tab in the Properties dialog will show you useful information about your document. In Word 6 you can access this by clicking on "Statistics" from the Summary Info dialog.

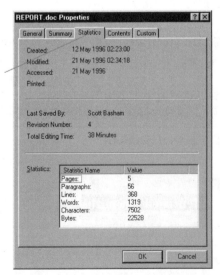

3 When you use the Open document dialog, you can click on the "Advanced" button to tell Word to search on the basis of the information entered in a document's properties.

Rulers and Tabulation

CHAPTER SIX

Text which is laid out with correct and accurate horizontal alignment greatly helps to give a document a professional look.

Effective use of white space, including tabulation, is one of the most important considerations when using a word-processor. This chapter deals with a range of tabulation features and examples.

Covers

Displaying Special Characters

There are various special characters such as spaces, carriage returns and tabs which, though normally invisible, all have an important effect on the document.

If you click on the ¶ button in the toolbar, the display will indicate where these characters are:

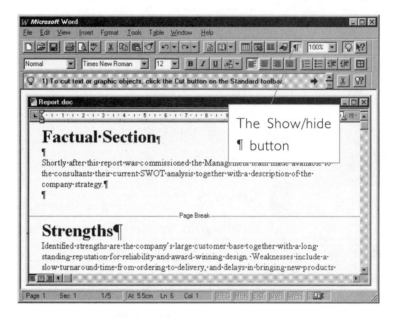

Spaces are shown as single dots (higher up than full stops), paragraph markers as ¶, and tab stops as right-pointing arrows.

Other hidden text such as field codes will also be displayed.

Default Tabulation

The default tab stops are set every half inch. When you press the Tab key, Word automatically moves across the page, stopping when it reaches the next tab stop position.

To see how this works:

1 Make sure that the ¶ button is active.

2 Enter items of text separated by a single tab character.

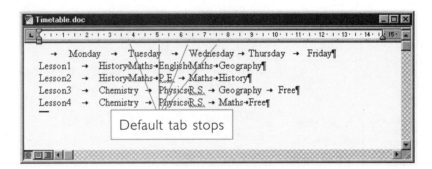

Default tab stops

Creating Your Own Tabulation

1 Select the text.

2 Click in the ruler to create a new tab (shaped like an "L") and drag to adjust its position.

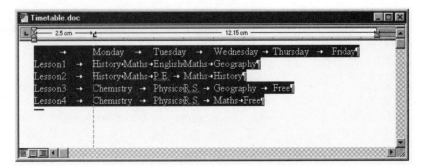

...contd

Any new tab stops you create will automatically override the default tabs.

3 Repeat this process to create more tab stops.

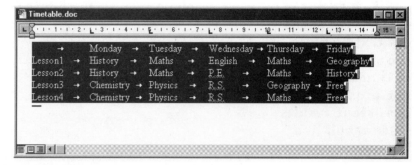

Deleting Tabs

You can delete your tab stops simply by dragging them downwards out of the Ruler.

Different Types of Tab

So far you've created left-aligned tabs, which cause text to align along its left edge under the tab stop.

You can move your own tab stops at any time by dragging them within the Ruler - but be sure to select the main text first.

1 Click the Tab Alignment button to change to centre tabs.

2 You can now create centred tabs by clicking in the Ruler:

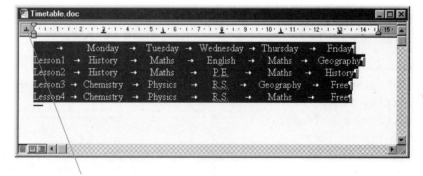

Tab Alignment button now showing centred tabs

As you click on the Tab Alignment button, it cycles between Left, Centre, Right and Decimal alignment.

...contd

Here is an example of right-aligned tabs:

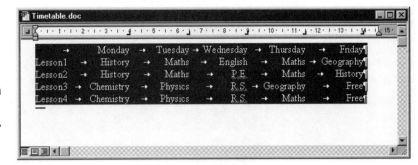

 Tabulation is a paragraph-level attribute. Each paragraph can have its own tab stops if necessary.

Decimal tabs are used to line up numbers along the decimal point:

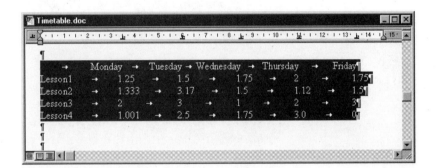

Usually a mixture of different tabs is required:

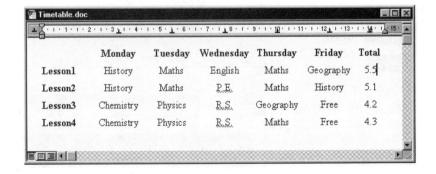

The Tabs Dialog Box

More options can be found in the Tabs dialog box.

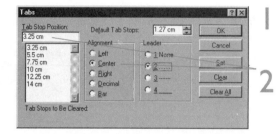

1 Choose "Tabs" from the Format menu.

2 Set the position and alignment of the tab.

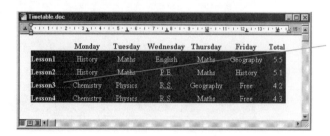

This example also uses a leader consisting of a row of dots.

Bar Tabs

These can only be accessed from the Tabs dialog box, as shown above. Setting a bar tab causes a vertical line to appear in the text at the specified position.

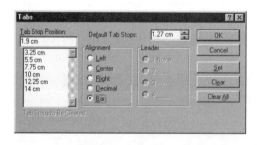

You can also access the Tabs dialog via the Paragraph dialog.

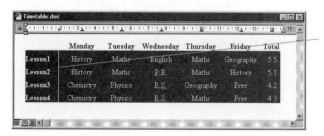

Bar tab

CHAPTER SEVEN

Lists, Headers and Footers

Word has many features which help you to avoid repetitive work. This chapter concentrates on lists and text which is repeated at the top and bottom of each page (headers and footers).

Covers

Creating a Bulleted List

Select the text to be bulleted.

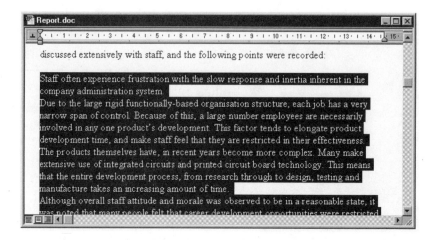

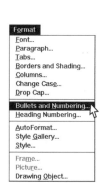

2 Choose "Bullets and Numbering" from the Format menu.

If necessary, click on
the "Bulleted" tab.

You can also select "Bullets and Numbering" from the pop-up menu which appears when you click in the document window with the right mouse button.

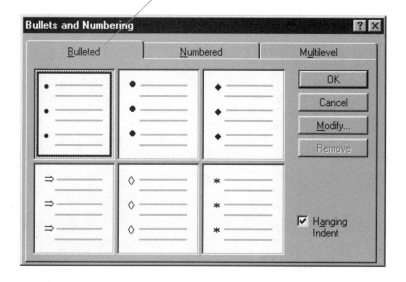

3 Choose the type of bullet text. Click on "Modify" to see further options...

...contd

The following dialog box appears:

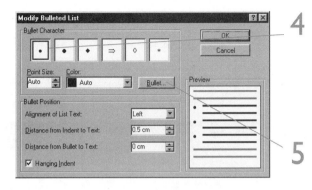

4 Choose the required settings. Click on the required bullet symbol...

5 ...or click here to select another from the complete range of characters.

7 Click "OK" to exit all dialogs.

6 Select the font and character.

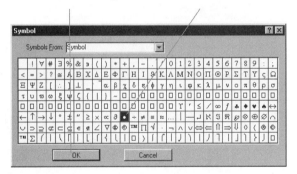

8 The selected text is now bulleted.

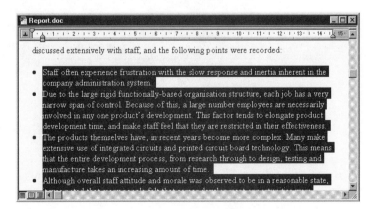

Creating a Numbered List

1 Select the text to be numbered.

2 Holding down the right mouse button, choose "Bullets and Numbering" from the pop-up menu.

3 If necessary, select the "Numbered" tab.

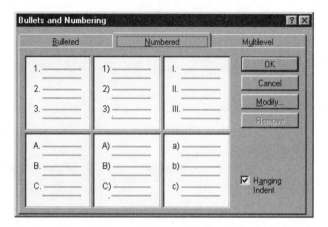

4 Choose a numbering style. Click on "Modify".

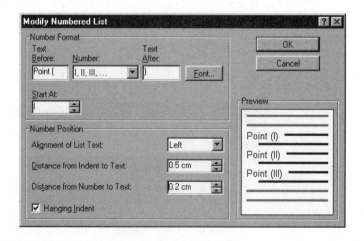

5 Experiment with different settings, referring to the Preview box to see the results.

6 Click "OK" to exit all dialog boxes.

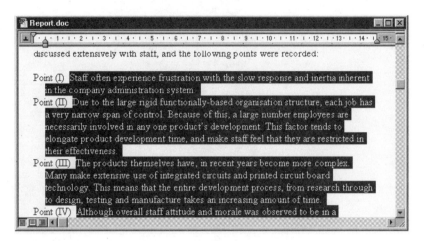

Multilevel Lists

Select the text, choose "Bullets and Numbering" as before, and activate the "Multilevel" tab.

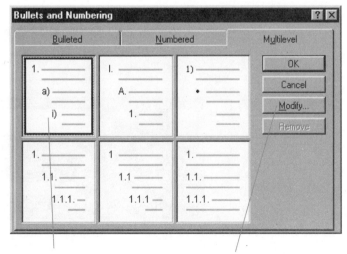

1 Either choose from the list of standard settings...

2 ...or use the "Modify" button to customise the list format.

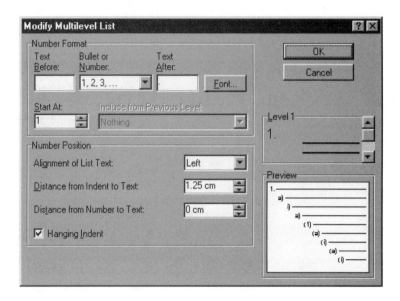

When you click "OK" the Multilevel settings will be applied to the text. Most lines become level 1 list entries. Any lines which begin with a single tab character become level 2 entries, lines which start with two tab characters become level 3 entries, and so on...

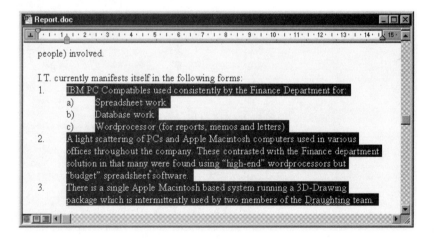

Headers and Footers

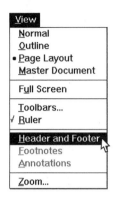

Headers normally appear at the top of every page, footers at the bottom (an example being "7. Lists, Headers and Footers" on this page).

Creating/Modifying a Header

1 Choose "Header and Footer" from the View menu.

Word will automatically change to Page Layout View. The main page text will be greyed out to let you concentrate on the header. The Header and Footer toolbar will also appear.

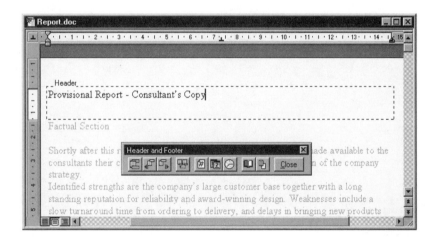

2 Enter the text and apply formatting as required.

The Header and Footer Toolbar

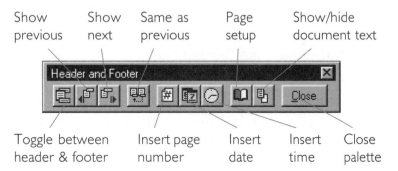

Show previous   Show next   Same as previous   Page setup   Show/hide document text

Toggle between header & footer   Insert page number   Insert date   Insert time   Close palette

Creating/Modifying a Footer

1 Click on the left-most button in the Header and Footer toolbar. This will take you to the footer text.

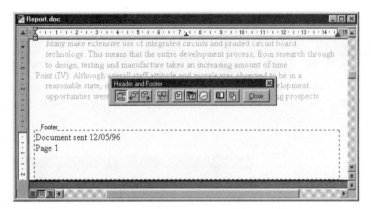

2 Enter the footer text. You can include automatic page numbers, or the current date or time by clicking on the relevant button in the toolbar.

3 Click "Close" when you've finished.

By default, the header and footer on a page will apply to all remaining pages in the document. You can override this by editing the headers/footers for other pages separately.

Now the header and footer text is greyed out, and you can edit the main text again. Note that the picture below shows Page Layout View. In Normal View headers and footers do not appear at all.

CHAPTER EIGHT

Automatic Features

Word has many automatic features which will operate on selected text or a complete document. This chapter looks at many of these, including search and replace tools and facilities for correction of spelling or grammar.

Covers

Find

Word can be instructed to search through your document for particular words, groups of characters, or formatting attributes.

You can set the Find dialog to look for text in particular case, for whole words (rather than groups of letters), to use wildcard searching, or phonetic matching.

1 Choose "Find" from the Edit menu, or type Control+F.

2 Enter your search text in the "Find What" box.

3 Set the search direction, either from the insertion point downwards, upwards or throughout the entire document.

4 If you want to make a search based on attributes, open the Format pop-up menu, and choose the relevant option(s).

In this example we're searching for Times New Roman 14-point text:

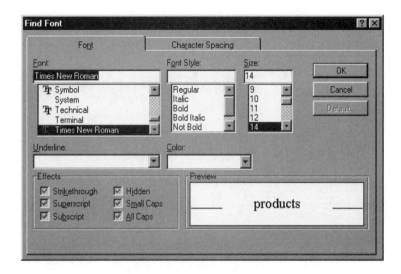

5 Click "OK" to return to the Find dialog, then click on the Find button to start the search.

Word highlights the first instance of text matching your search criteria:

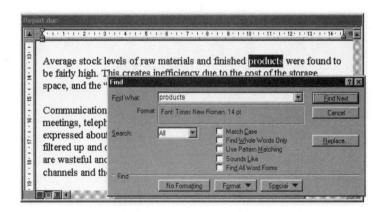

6 Click on Find Next to continue searching for subsequent instances of text matching the same search criteria.

Replace

This works in the same way as Find, but with additional facilities for automatically substituting new text and/or formatting.

| Choose Replace from the Edit menu, or type Control+H.

There is a button in the Find dialog which takes you directly to the Replace dialog.

This changes from "Find" to "Replace" according to context.

2 Enter the "Find" text, then use the Format pop-up menu to set any text attributes.

3 Enter the "Replace with" text. Note that, as soon as you click in the "Replace with" box, the lower section of the dialog box switches from "Find" to "Replace". You can now set the Replace attributes if necessary.

Special Characters

Example 1

If "Find Whole Words Only" were active, entering 19^#^# in the Find box would instruct Word to locate any instances of the characters "19" followed by two digits. So it would locate "1901" and "1999" but not "1899" or "19101".

You can use the "Special" pop-up menu in the Replace dialog box to easily insert the keyboard codes for special characters. In this example we're looking for two consecutive line breaks, and replacing with a single line break.

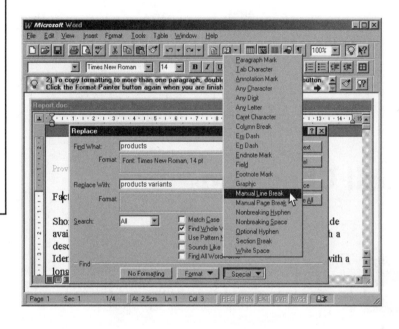

Example 2

If you entered:
Windows
in the Find box, and then:
Microsoft ^& *95*
under Replace, then all instances of "Windows" would change to "Microsoft Windows 95".

These special codes, also available from the "Special" pop-up menu, act like wildcards, allowing Word to find text which varies according to some structure:

Find Wildcards

^?   Any character

^#   Any digit

^$ Any letter

^w   White space

Replace Codes

^&   Reinsert the "Find What" text (see example in margin).

^onnn ANSII or ASCII character

^c   Clipboard contents

Pattern Matching

If you activate "Pattern matching" in the Find or Replace dialog, you can set up more sophisticated searches.

A Simple Example

Typing "[a-g]" will now indicate any character in the range "a" through to "g", so entering "196[4-9]" would match with "1964", "1965", "1966", "1967", "1968" and "1969".

More Complex Examples

When working inside the Find or Replace dialog, press the F1 key and click on "Advanced Search Criteria" for a full list of the options including explanations and examples.

Spell Checking

| If you don't want to spell check your entire document, then select only the text you require.

The shortcut key for Spell Checking is F7.

2 Choose "Spelling" from the Tools menu, or click on the Spell Check icon:

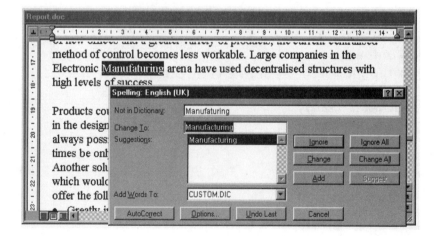

...contd

This message appears when Word has finished checking through the document.

You can make Word change or ignore all instances of the current text by clicking "Ignore All" or "Change All".

You can also access the Spelling Options dialog from the Tools menu.

3 When a suspect word is found, you can:

- Click "Change" to replace it with Word's suggestion.
- Select another entry from the list of suggestions, and click "Change".
- Enter your own correction and click "Change".
- Click "Ignore" if the word is correct (e.g. a proper noun).

4 If you enter your own correction and would like the word to be added to the dictionary, click the "Add" button.

5 You can change the dictionary file by selecting from the "Add words to" pop-up menu.

6 Clicking the "Options" button takes you to the "Spelling" tab of the Options dialog box:

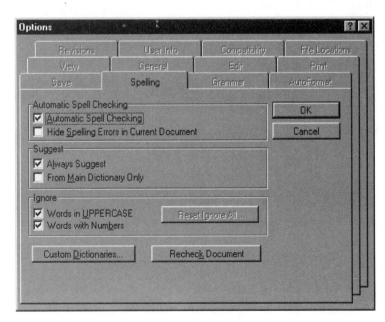

Word Count

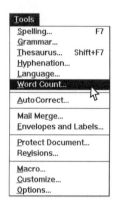

1 To count the words in one area only, select it in the normal way, otherwise the entire document will be scanned.

2 Choose "Word Count" from the Tools menu:

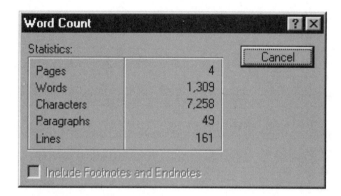

Thesaurus

1 Select the word to be used.

2 Press Shift+F7 or choose "Thesaurus" from the Tools menu:

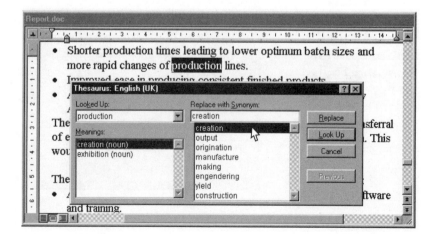

AutoCorrect

Many of us make the same spelling or typing mistakes again and again.

We can instruct Word to automatically substitute the correction:

| Choose AutoCorrect from the Tools menu:

Word 7 contains a greater number of corrections including common mistakes for "necessary", "occasion", and transposition errors such as "knwo" instead of "know". You can browse through these from the AutoCorrect dialog.

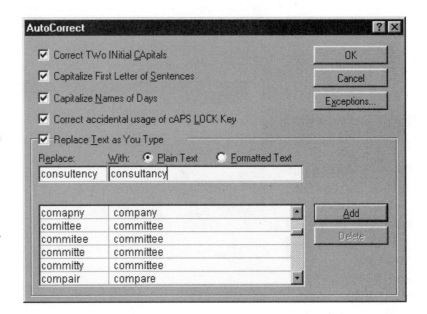

2 Enter the mistake, the correction, then click on the Add button.

3 Now when you type, Word spots the error and substitutes automatically:

refer to the consultency|	…	refer to the consultancy|
original text typed		*corrected by Word*

You can now continue through the rest of your life completely unaware that you are consistently failing to spell correctly.

AutoText

This is a less automatic version of AutoCorrect, and is useful for setting up your own abbreviations.

If you find that you often need to type the same text, then it would be worth setting up an AutoText entry:

Creating an AutoText Entry

1. Type the text and select it.

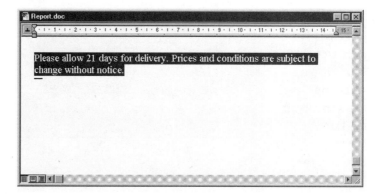

HANDY TIP

You can also use the AutoText toolbar button. If it isn't visible, you can add it to a toolbar by choosing "Customise" from the Toolbar pop-up menu (accessed by holding down the right mouse button over a toolbar).

2. Choose AutoText from the Edit menu.

The selected text is automatically inserted into the "Selection" area of the AutoText dialog box.

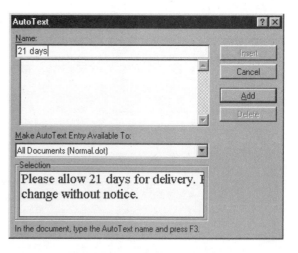

3. Edit the "Name" box to the abbreviation you require. Click "OK".

...contd

Using AutoText

1 Simply type the abbreviation:

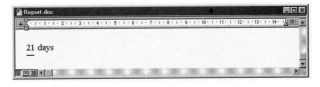

You can also insert AutoText using the "AutoText" command from the Edit menu. This gives you the option of inserting the text with its original formatting intact.

2 Press F3 or the AutoText icon in the toolbar.

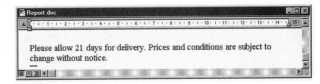

The abbreviation is inflated back into the original text.

The Spike

The Spike is a temporary piece of AutoText which can be added to with a single key command.

Creating a Spike

1 Select some text and type Control+F3.

The text disappears. It has been impaled on the Spike.

2 Repeat the process with a second piece of text.

You can repeat this more times if necessary. Each time you press Control+F3 any selected text is put onto the Spike.

3 Finally, place the Insertion Point at the destination for the text and press Control+Shift+F3.

The text is pulled off the Spike and placed back into the document.

Hyphenation

1 You can change the hyphenation options for your document by choosing "Hyphenation" from the Tools menu:

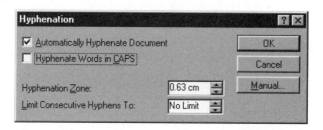

2 If you click on the "Manual" button you can review hyphenation manually throughout your document:

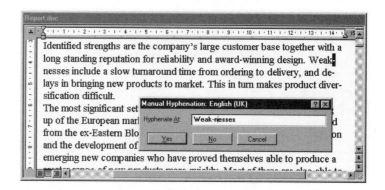

HANDY TIP **You can also override hyphen-ation for individual paragraphs by clicking on the "Don't hyphenate" button in the Text Flow tab of the Paragraph dialog box.**

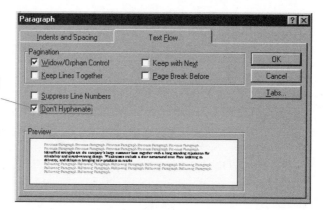

Grammar Checking

1 Choose "Grammar" from the Tools menu:

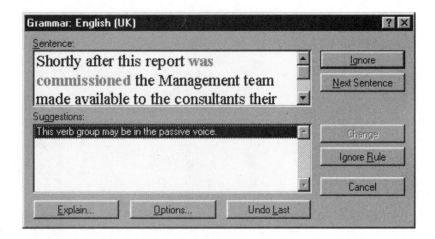

2 Click the Explain button to find out about the guideline or rule you may have broken.

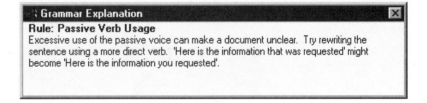

The default setup of Word 7 doesn't include the Grammar checker. If you need to install this then run the Word 7 setup program once again and choose Add/ Remove Components. The Grammar checker is listed under "Microsoft Word Proofing Tools".

A different approach to grammar is required for different types of document:

3 Click on the Options button from the Grammar dialog box. If you are currently working in the document then you can access this directly by choosing "Options" from the Tools menu and then the "Grammar" tab.

The following dialog box appears:

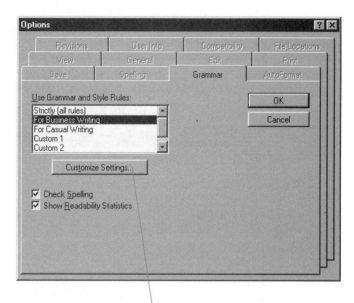

4 You can tailor the grammar checking to your own
requirements by clicking on the "Customize Settings" button:

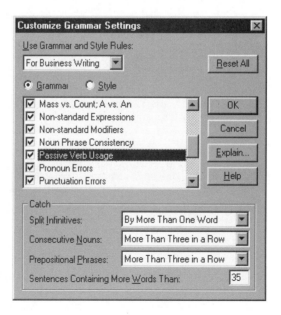

When deciding on what to use, it may be worth clicking on the "Explain" button to help you determine the usefulness of a rule:

Although present in Word 6, both "Sexist Expressions" and "Pretentious Words" seem to be absent from Word 7's list of grammatical rules.

Readability Statistics

When the Grammar Check is over, Word displays the Readability Statistics information:

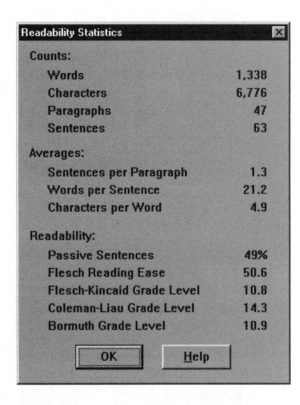

Unfortunately no one has, as yet, figured out a way of automatically analysing the boredom level of a document. This is one job still left to us lucky humans.

The Flesch Reading Ease value is in the range 0...100, increasing with ease of reading. Standard text rates between 60 and 70.

The Grade Level values give an indication as to the school grade appropriate for your text. For example, a level of 3 means that it would be understandable by someone in the third grade or below. Standard text normally weighs in between 7 and 8.

CHAPTER NINE

Styles

Styles help you to easily apply a consistent set of formatting commands to main text, headings and other elements of your document.

Once you start using styles, you'll be able to control your document's presentation with the minimum of tedious manual editing.

Covers

Using the Default Styles

A style is a complete collection of type attributes saved under a single name. There are two main benefits to this:

- Your document will have a visual consistency if, for example, all your subheadings look the same.

- You can quickly make drastic but coherent changes to the format of your document by redefining the styles already used by the text.

Applying a Style

1 Select the text.

2 Select a style from the pop-up menu:

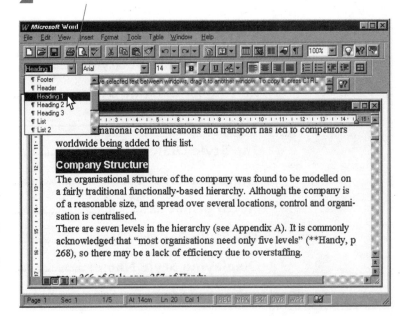

HANDY TIP **The keyboard shortcut for this is Control+Shift+S. Then type the first few letters of the style and press the down arrow key.**

The text has now been set to this style. Whenever you select text on the page, the pop-up menu will indicate which style is currently being used.

By default all text starts off using the style "Normal".

Editing an Existing Style

1 Select some text in the document which already uses the style to be changed.

2 Use the toolbar and menus as normal to experiment with changes in formatting.

3 When you are happy with the changes, reselect the style from the pop-up list and press Return:

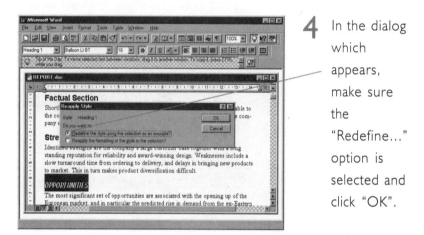

4 In the dialog which appears, make sure the "Redefine..." option is selected and click "OK".

All text in the document using this style will now change automatically...

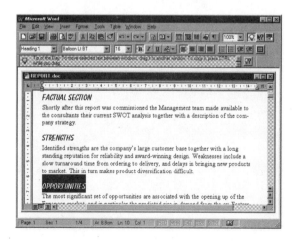

Creating a New Style

| Format the text as normal in the document.

2 When you are happy with its appearance, enter the new style name in the pop-up menu and press return:

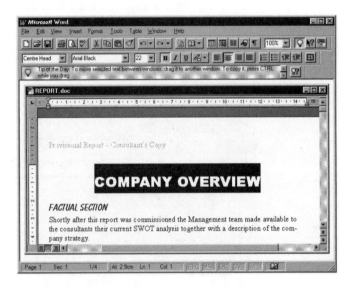

The new style is automatically created, and can now be applied to other text.

The Style Dialog Box

Choose "Style" from the Format menu, or alternatively press Control+Shift+S twice (pressing this once takes you to the pop-up menu).

The dialog box which appears lets you preview and manage all the styles:

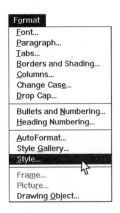

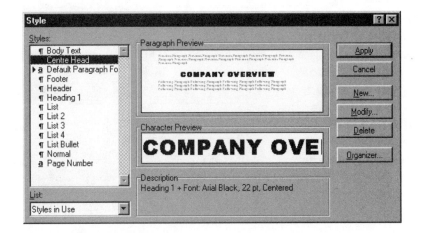

Creating a New Style Using The Dialog Boxes

Click on the "New" button in the Style dialog box.

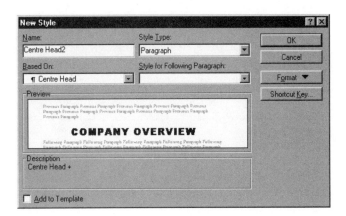

From this dialog you can put together the style definition.

Setting a Keyboard Shortcut for a Style

┃ Click the "Shortcut Key" button in the Style dialog box.

Word tells you if your proposed shortcut key is currently being used for something else. If you go ahead, then your style shortcut will override the previous setting.

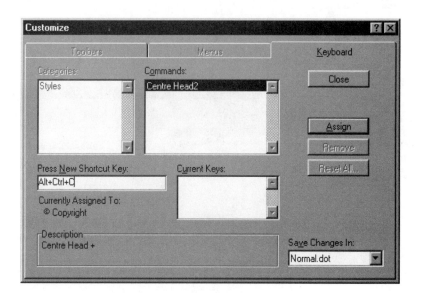

2 Enter the shortcut key for the style and click the "Assign" button. You can repeat this process to add more than one keyboard shortcut for the same style.

3 When you have finished, click the "Close" button to return to the previous dialog box.

Setting the Format

Back in the New Style dialog box, select "Font" from the "Format" pop-up menu:

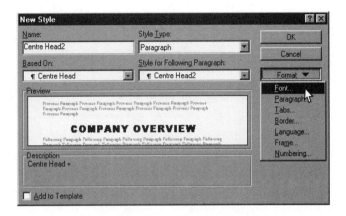

This will take you to the Font dialog box. When you have finished making the settings you may also want to use the "Format" pop-up menu to set other attributes such as Paragraph.

2 Click "OK". The new style is added to the list.

Modifying a Style

From the Styles dialog box, click on "Modify".

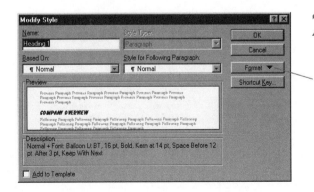

2 Use the Format button to make the desired changes, then click "OK".

Character-level Styles

Normally styles operate on a paragraph level, i.e. they only apply to whole paragraphs.

To create a character-level style:

1 Choose "New" from the Style dialog.

2 Select "Character" from the "Style Type" pop-up menu:

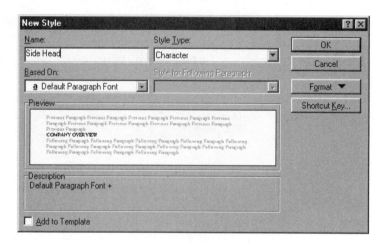

3 Use the "Format" pop-up to set the character level attributes:

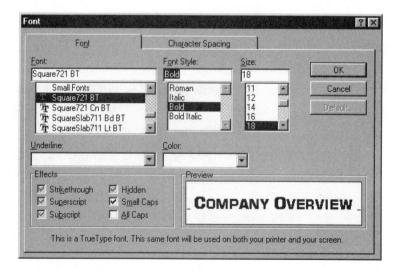

You can now apply your character style to individual words or phrases without affecting the entire surrounding paragraph.

If text already uses a paragraph style, then the character style will override these settings:

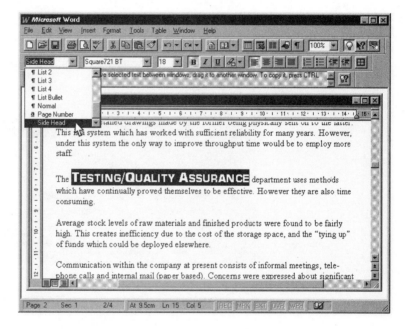

Word 7 Style Names

In Word 7, character-level style names appear in the pop-up list prefixed with **a**. Paragraph styles appear prefixed with **¶**.

Word 6 Style Names

In Word 6, character-level style names appear as normal text in any style list, whereas paragraph-level style names are in bold.

AutoFormat

If you have created a document using no styles or even ordinary formatting, then AutoFormat can attempt to take care of this for you.

The AutoFormat icon

I   Either click on the AutoFormat icon in the toolbar or, if you want to monitor the changes, choose "AutoFormat" from the Format menu.

2   Click "OK" to start the process. The following dialog will then appear:

3   To manually review and authorise changes, click on the "Review Changes" button;
or
To control the overall look of the document, click on "Style Gallery".

The Style Gallery

1 You can activate the Style Gallery dialog either via the AutoFormat dialog or directly from the Format menu.

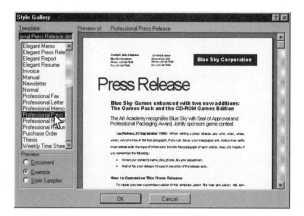

2 Choose a Template design, then a preview option. "Document" shows you how your document would look with the proposed style definitions. "Example" shows you an example document demonstrating the different styles.

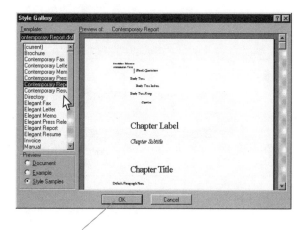

"Samples" lists each style name using its own attributes.

3 Click "OK" if you want your document to adopt these new style definitions.

Displaying Style Names

Sometimes it is useful to see instantly which styles are being used by the paragraphs in your document.

1 Make sure that Normal View is active (you can set this using the View menu or the icon at the bottom left of the screen).

2 Choose "Options" from the Tools menu.

3 Click on the View tab.

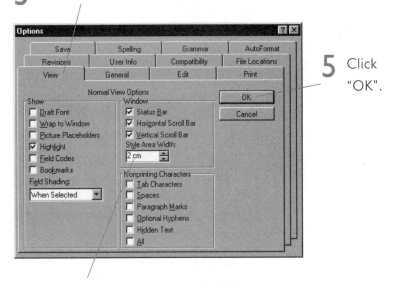

5 Click "OK".

4 Set the "Style Area Width" to a figure greater than zero.

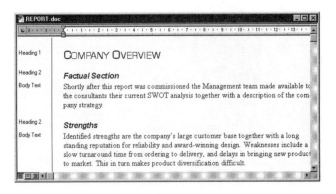

In this example we've used a 2cm margin area in which to list the styles used.

CHAPTER TEN

Templates and Wizards

Templates act as blueprints for standard types of document which you would need to use again and again. Examples may be standard memos, reports, letters or faxes. A Wizard is a "live" document which guides you through its own design.

This chapter shows you how to use Templates and Wizards, customise a Template for your own purposes, or create a new Template.

Covers

Using Templates

A Template contains a range of settings to be used as a starting point for a new document.

If you use the "New" icon instead of the File menu, Word uses the "Blank Document" or "Normal" Template.

The Normal Template

1 Choose "New" from the File menu:

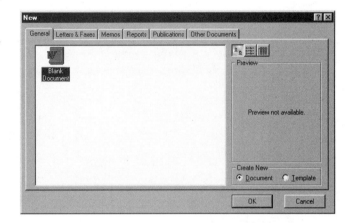

Word lists the Templates available. Often you'll use the simple "Blank Document" Template.

In Word 6 you'll see a simpler text-based list of available Templates and Wizards:

2 Click on the other tabs to see more available Templates.

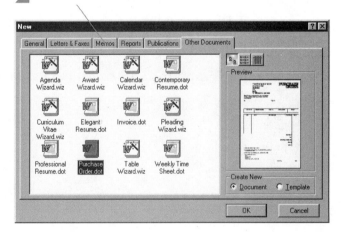

3 Leave the option as "Blank Document" and click "OK".

Form Templates

1 Choose "New" from the File menu.

2 Select the "Other Documents" Tab.

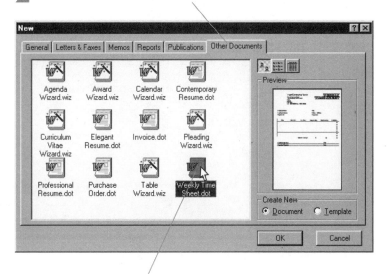

3 Click on "Weekly Time Sheet" and click "OK".

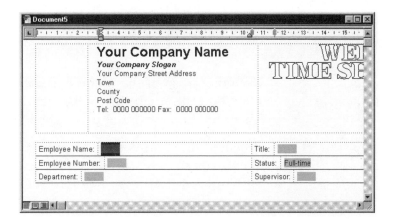

Form Filling

"Weekly Time Sheet" contains a complete design for a weekly time sheet form. Forms normally contain fields, which can be easily filled in or edited without disturbing the surrounding text.

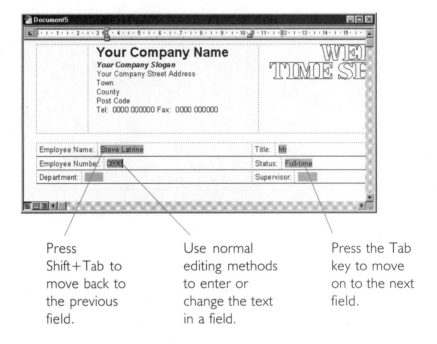

Press Shift+Tab to move back to the previous field.

Use normal editing methods to enter or change the text in a field.

Press the Tab key to move on to the next field.

Note that most of the menu options are greyed out, and that you cannot edit the main text in the document. You're restricted to editing the fields, saving and printing.

Provided the Template is set exactly the way you want, this allows you to easily produce forms without being distracted by Word's vast array of features and controls.

...contd

Changing the Form

1 Go to the Tools menu and choose "Unprotect Document".

2 You can now fully edit the document, adapting it to your own ends:

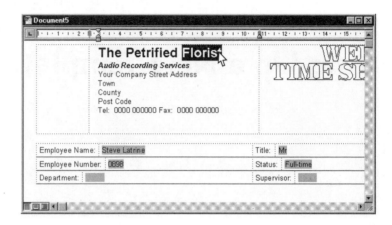

Template Defaults

Defaults are settings which are used initially when you create a new document or add new text.

1 Open the Font dialog box.

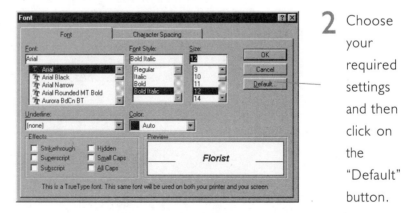

2 Choose your required settings and then click on the "Default" button.

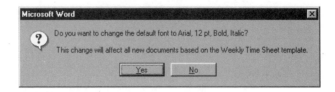

3 If you click "Yes", the font information will be saved into the currently used Template document.

Setting Up a New Template

Any document can be saved as a Template, but in this example you'll return to your form from earlier on.

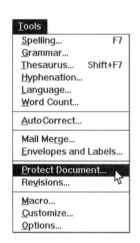

1 Select "Protect Document" from the Tools menu.

2 Set the Protect option to "Forms".

Note that you only need to do this if the Template is to be used as a form.

3 Choose "Save" from the File menu:

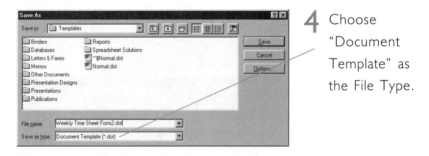

4 Choose "Document Template" as the File Type.

The document will automatically be saved with a .DOT extension within Word's Template directory.

Changing Styles in a Template

When you open a document, Word uses the Styles built into the Template selected.

As we saw earlier, you can alter these Styles for individual documents using the "Style" command from the Format menu.

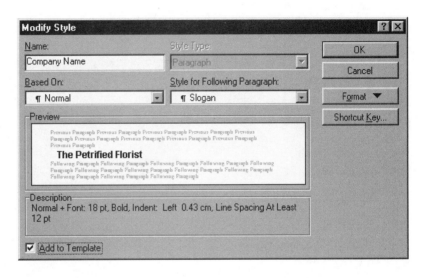

BEWARE

If you record a style change to the "Blank Document" or "Normal" Template, this will affect most new documents.

To copy a style change back into the Template itself, click on "Add to Template" in the Modify Style dialog box.

The Templates and Add-ins Dialog

Word always keeps track of the Template used to create a document. It is possible to change this even after you've started work:

1 If necessary, unprotect your document (Tools menu).

2 Choose "Templates" from the File menu.

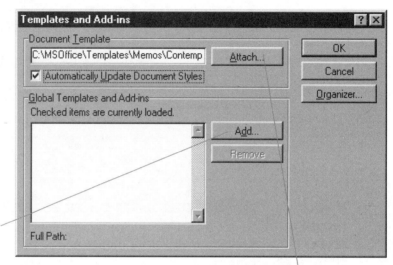

HANDY TIP

You can use the "Add" button to make available styles stored in other Templates. Any Templates listed in the "Global" box are always available.

3 Use the "Attach" button to attach a new Template. If you select "Automatically Update Document Styles" then the Styles from the new Template will be reapplied to the document text.

Wizards

Wizard documents are alive; they actually build and design themselves. They do this by asking you a series of questions when you create a new file based on a Wizard Template.

An example

1   Go to the File menu and choose "New".

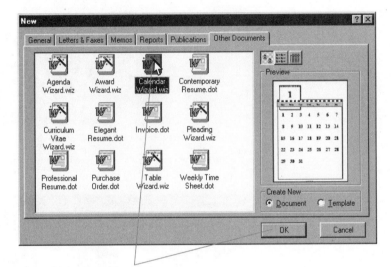

2   Select the "Other Documents" tab then "Calendar Wizard" and click "OK".

3   Select "Portrait" orientation and click the "Next" button.

4   Select the "Banner" style and click on "Next".

5 Select "Yes" to include a picture and click "Next".

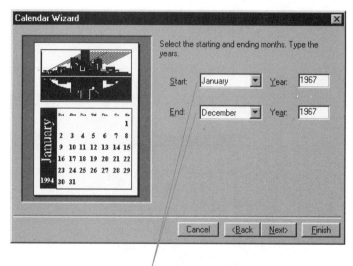

6 Enter the range of dates and click "Next".

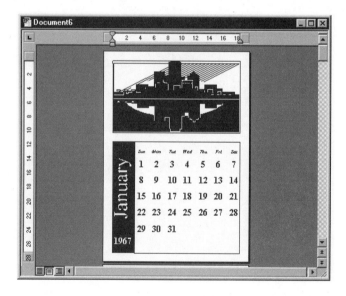

You now have a complete calendar document ready for editing, saving and printing.

CHAPTER ELEVEN

Graphical Features

Although not a fully-blown graphics package, Word contains a comprehensive collection of clipart as well as a respectable range of graphical editing features. This chapter takes you through the processes involved with incorporating pictures and illustrations into your document.

Covers

Using Clipart

Word has its own directory of clipart illustrations.

1 Click the Insertion Point at the destination for the graphic.

2 Choose "Picture" from the Insert menu.

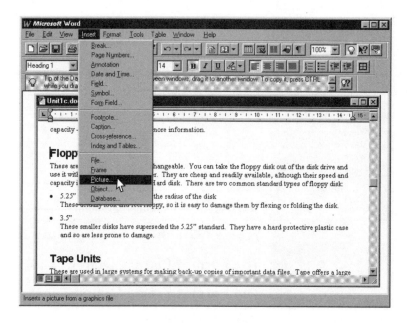

3 Locate the file you require and click "OK".

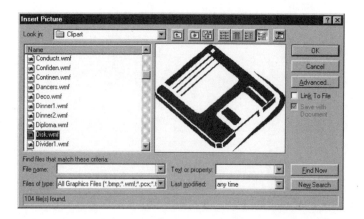

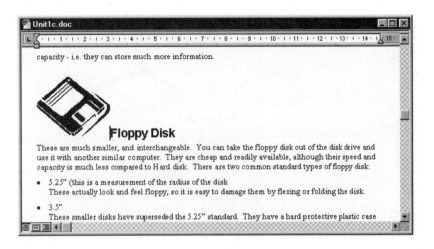

The picture is inserted as if it were a large character.

Manipulating Graphics

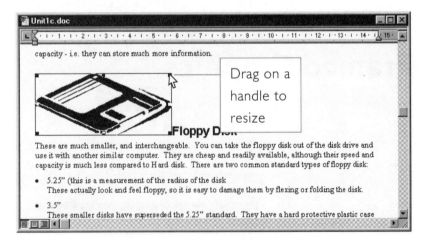

Drag on a handle to resize

| Click on the graphic to make its handles appear.

The handles are eight small square blocks which allow you to change the graphic's dimensions.

2 Drag on a handle to resize the picture.

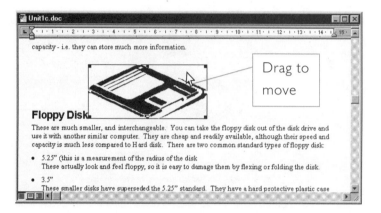

3 Drag anywhere within the object to move it to a new position.

Note that the graphic is treated like a text item, so when you drag it to a new position, the surrounding text moves to make room.

Framed Graphics

1 Select the picture.

2 Click on the Insert Frame icon in the Forms toolbar, or choose "Frame" from the Insert menu.

The graphic now inhabits a frame, and is no longer part of the text. The text flows around the frame.

The Format Picture Dialog

| 1 | Select the picture. | 2 | Choose "Picture" from the Format menu. |

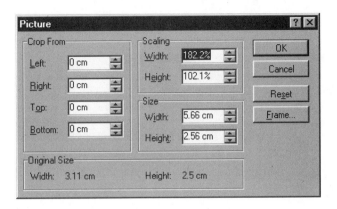

From here you can numerically alter the scale, size and crop parameters of the picture.

The Format Frame Dialog

| | Select the frame and choose "Frame" from the Format menu to change the frame options. |

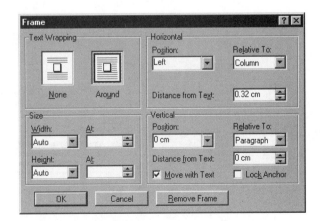

You can adjust the text wrap, and the frame's position in relation to the neighbouring paragraph.

Cropping a Picture

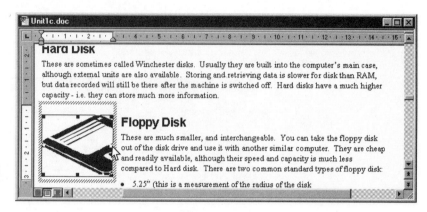

HANDY TIP

To abandon any cropping and restore a picture to its original size, select the picture, then choose "Picture" from the Format menu. Now click "Reset", then "OK".

To crop (i.e. cut away part of a picture), simply drag inwards on one of its handles while holding down the Shift key.

Cropping is non-destructive. This means that you can restore the rest of the picture by Shift-dragging outwards on a handle.

Frame Borders and Shading

Select the frame and choose "Borders and Shading" from the Format menu.

HANDY TIP

You can also use the Borders toolbar to change these features.

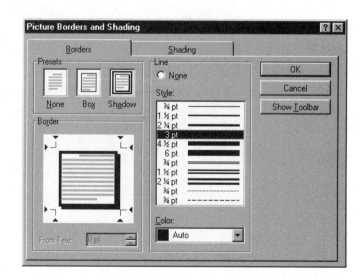

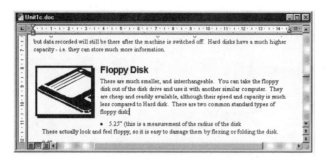

This example illustrates the shadow border effect.

Inserting a Blank Frame

1 With nothing selected, click on the Insert Frame icon.

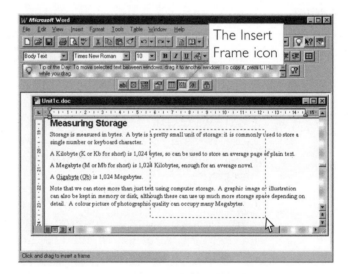

The Insert Frame icon

2 Click and drag over the frame area.

A new blank frame is created. You can fill this with text or graphics. Simply click inside to enter and format text as normal.

...contd

HANDY TIP

To prevent your document becoming too large, click on the "Link to File" checkbox. This means Word will not include the graphic data as part of the document, but instead access the original file when necessary.

3 To insert an image select the blank frame, choose "Picture" from the Insert menu and locate the desired file.

The picture appears in the frame.

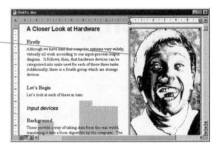

Types of Graphic File

Word can import many types of graphic file format. WMF, CGM, WPG, DRW, EPS and PCT files normally contain Draw-type objects which can be scaled up or down with no loss in quality, because they are stored as mathematical objects.

On the other hand BMP, PCX, TIF and GIF files are bitmapped: the image is stored as a structure of tiny dots/blocks. Be careful not to enlarge these pictures too much, or the dots will become very noticeable, causing a marked deterioration in quality.

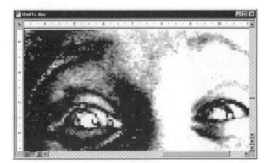

CHAPTER TWELVE

The Drawing Tools

Word's comprehensive drawing facilities are well integrated into the main package. In this chapter, you will see how easy it is to create your own drawings directly within the pages of your document.

Covers

Starting To Draw

To begin using Word's drawing facilities, click on the Drawing icon in the toolbar.

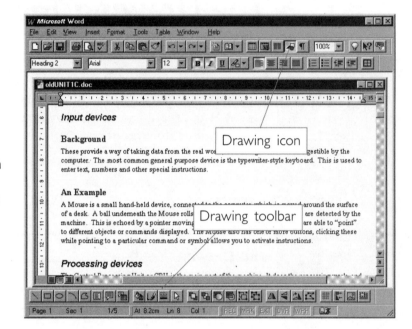

HANDY TIP You can also access this from the "Toolbars" option in the view menu, or by holding down the right mouse button on an existing toolbar.

The Drawing toolbar appears at the bottom of the screen. You can now draw on your page, either in a blank area or directly over the text.

The Drawing Toolbar

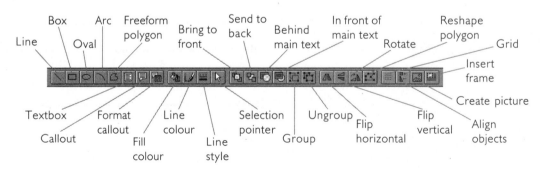

Creating Shapes

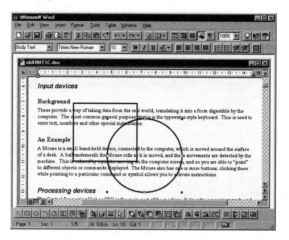

1 Select the appropriate shape tool.

2 Click and drag within the document to create the shape. For lines drag from one endpoint to the other; for boxes and ovals drag diagonally from one corner to the other.

3 Click on a shape with the Selection Pointer to select. Then you can drag it to another location, or resize by dragging directly on one of the shape's handles.

Lines and Fills

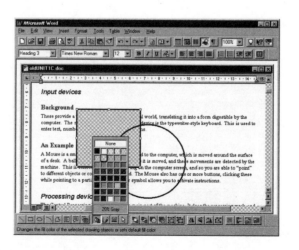

Click on a shape then use the Fill and Line icons to select colour, shading and line thickness.

Formatting Shapes

Select a shape then hold down the right mouse button to access the "Format Drawing Object" command from the pop-up menu.

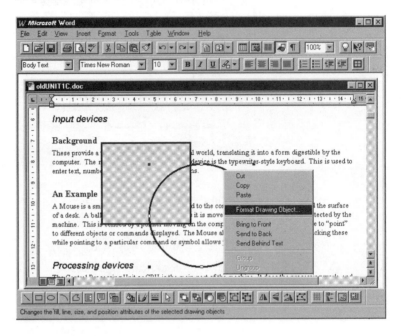

The Fill Tab

Use this to set the object's fill attributes. Use the Preview box for reference.

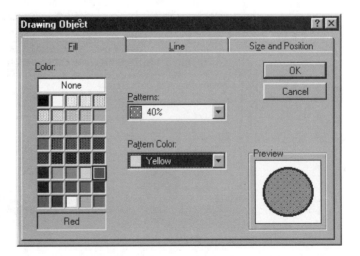

The Line Tab

From here you can set the object's line options such as colour, thickness and shadow effect.

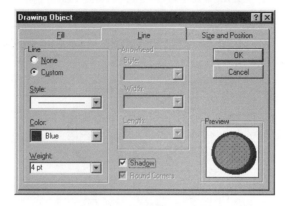

The Size and Position Tab

Here you can numerically control an object's size and position in relation to the adjacent paragraph of text.

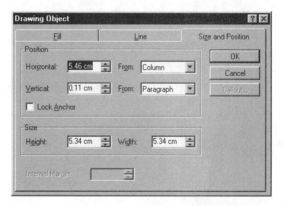

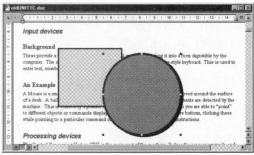

Front and Back

First select a shape, then use the Front and Back icons to move it in front of or behind the other drawing shapes.

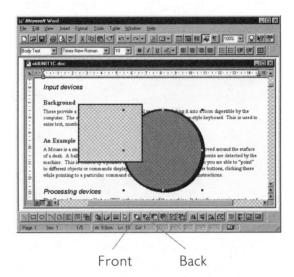

Front   Back

Selecting Multiple Objects

You can also select more than one object at a time by holding down Shift as you click. Shift-clicking a second time will deselect an object.

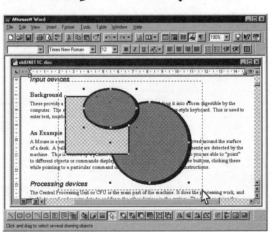

Click and drag with the pointer tool (starting in a blank space) to create a selection box. When you release the button, all objects completely ensnared will be selected.

In this example three objects were selected, then the Format Drawing Object option (from the right-hand mouse button pop-up menu) was used. A line style of "none" and a fill of grey were applied. The previous shadow effect was turned off.

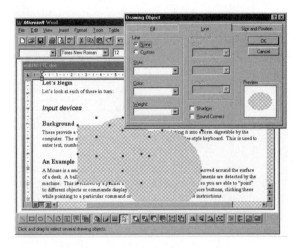

Send Behind the Text Layer

You can send objects either in front of or behind the main text in the document by clicking on these toolbar icons:

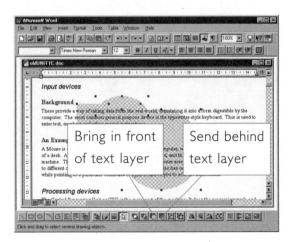

Aligning Objects

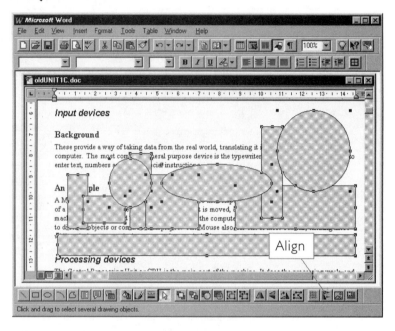

1 Select the objects to be aligned.

2 Click on the Align icon.

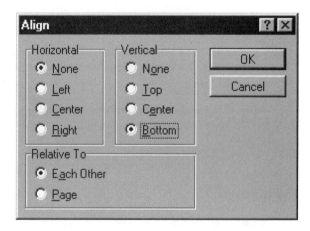

3 Select the Align options and click "OK".

In this example "Vertical/Bottom" alignment was used to align these objects relative to each other.

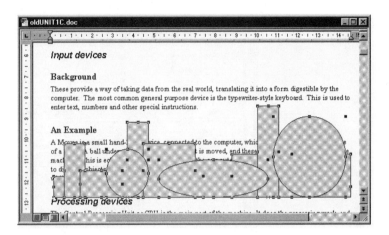

Group/Ungroup

HANDY TIP

Once objects are combined into a group, they can be treated as a single element. In this example the handles were used to stretch the entire shape.

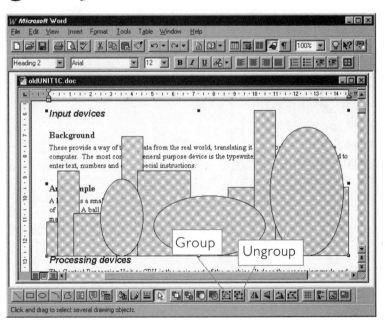

Use the Group tool to combine elements; Ungroup reverses this process.

In this example, after the grouped shape was stretched, the Line Colour button was used to set a line style of "none".

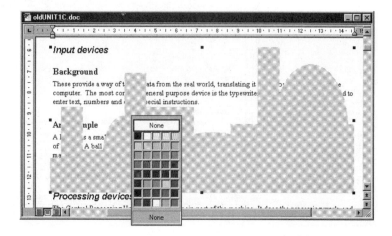

Finally, the grouped object was sent behind the text layer.

You can also send an object behind the text layer using the right mouse button menu.

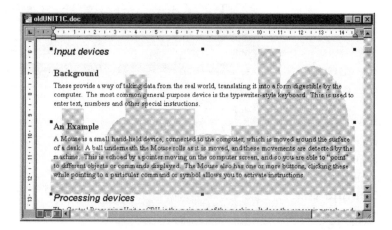

Cut, Copy and Paste

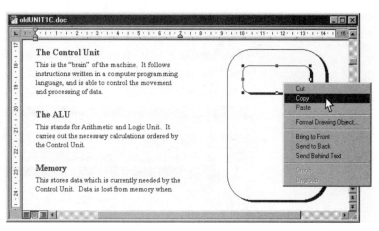

REMEMBER

Keyboard shortcuts for Cut, Copy and Paste are Control+X, Control+C, and Control+V respectively.

REMEMBER

If you chose Cut rather than Copy, the original shape would be removed.

1 Select an object.

2 Choose "Copy" from the right hand mouse button pop-up menu.

3 Choose "Paste" from the same menu.

Snap To Grid
Use the Snap to Grid feature to help you position elements easily.

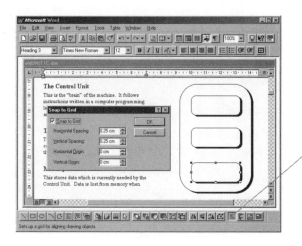

Snap to Grid

Callout Boxes

Callout boxes are useful ways of annotating a diagram. With the Callout box tool active, click/drag to create the line leading into the box. You can then move or resize the box, and enter its text.

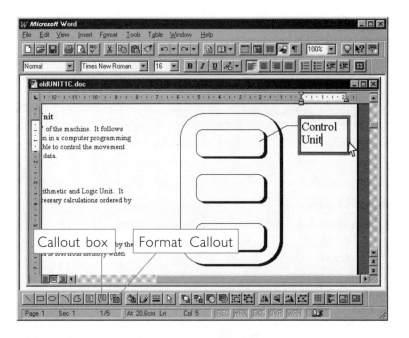

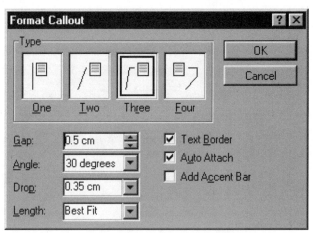

The Format Callout icon lets you customise the Callout box options.

Freeform Polygons

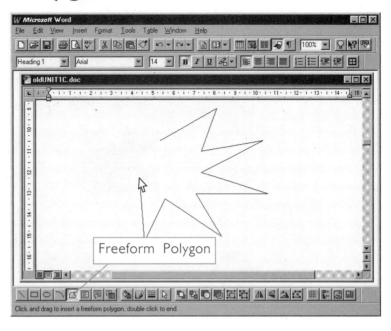

Freeform Polygon

If you drag (instead of click) with the Polygon tool, you create a freeform wavy line.

1 Select the Freeform Polygon tool.

2 Click on each point in turn.

3 Click back on the start point to complete a closed shape. If you don't want it closed then double-click to end.

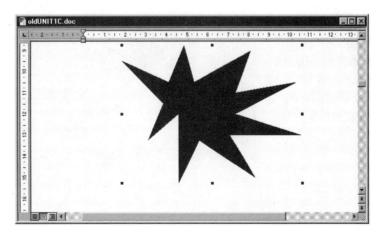

Reshaping a Polygon

1 Select the polygon and click on the Reshape icon.

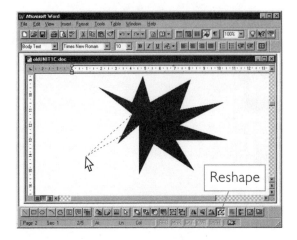

Reshape

2 Drag to move the corner points.

3 Control-click on part of the line to create a new point.

4 Control-click directly on a point to delete.

Creating a Picture

Use this tool to make the selected object(s) into a picture.

HANDY TIP

Note that here the Drawing toolbar has repositioned to the middle of the screen. All toolbars can be moved in this way simply by dragging with the mouse.

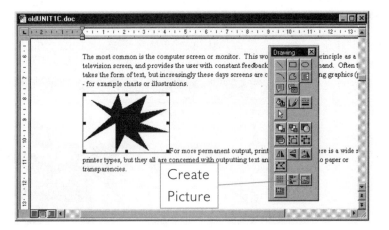

Create Picture

Editing an Imported Picture

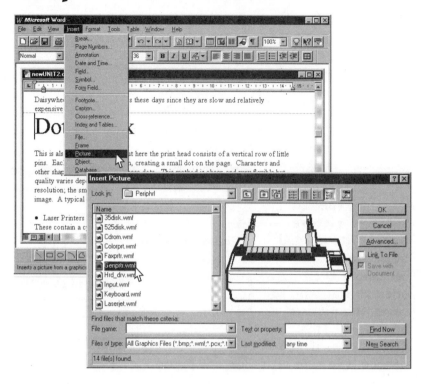

Import a clipart picture as normal, using the "Picture" option from the Insert menu.

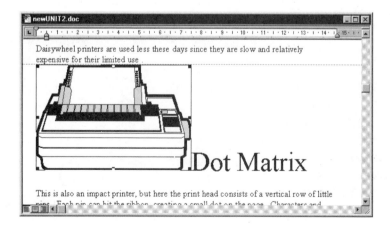

...contd

2 Double-click on the Picture.

A new Draw window opens.

3 Edit the shape. In this example we ungrouped, applied a grey fill, moved one polygon and reshaped another:

 If you extend the picture beyond its normal bounding rectangle then click this button to reset the picture boundary. This also applies if you reduce it in size.

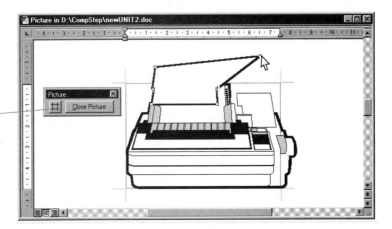

4 Click on "Close" in the floating palette.

This returns you to the Word document.

 You can add a caption to a picture by choosing "Caption" from the Insert menu.

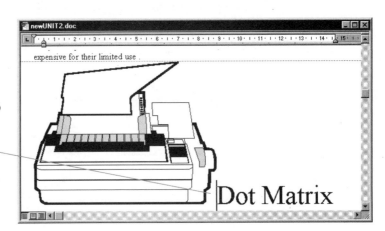

CHAPTER THIRTEEN

WordArt Special Effects

WordArt is another mini-application included with Word. It allows you to apply a wide range of special graphical effects to type. This chapter shows you how to access WordArt and experiment with its options.

The Insert Object method used to invoke WordArt can also be used to activate other applications (such as MS Excel) which are OLE-compatible.

Covers

Insert Object

WordArt interfaces with Word using OLE (Object Linking and Embedding). Any application which supports OLE (e.g. Microsoft Excel or PowerPoint) will work in the same way.

| Choose "Object" from the Insert menu.

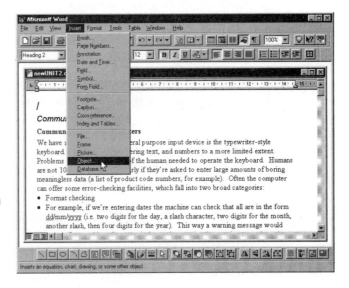

REMEMBER

WordArt is an added application included with Word. However, in Word 7 it is not part of the default installation. If you need to install WordArt, re-run the Word Setup program and choose "Add/ Remove Components". WordArt can be found under the section called "Office Tools".

2 Choose "Microsoft WordArt" from the Object Type list.

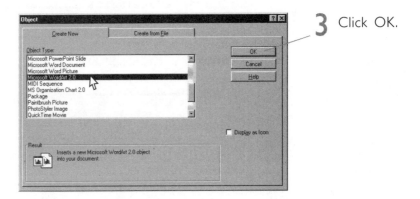

3 Click OK.

Microsoft WordArt will then take control.

Entering Text

Enter your text in the floating window:

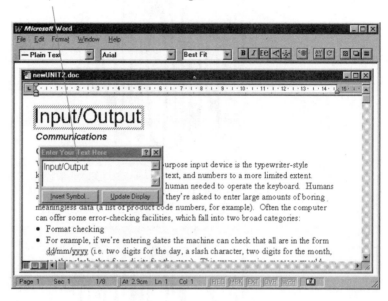

Choosing an Effect

Select a text effect from the drop-down list.

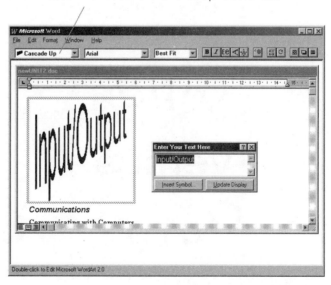

Example Effects

Triangle (Inverted)

Circle (Pour)

Wave2

Inflate (Top)

Button (Curve)

Fade Up

The Special Effects Box

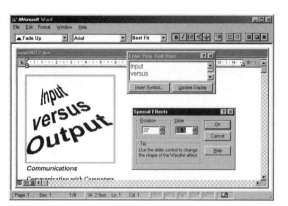

Choose "Rotation and Effects" from the Format menu.

 HANDY TIP

Most of these options are also accessible from the WordArt toolbar at the top of the window area.

Spacing Between Characters

Adjust the horizontal distance between characters with this dialog box, which can also be accessed from the Format menu.

Shading

"Shading", another option from the Format menu, is useful if you don't want the text solid black.

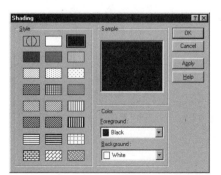

Shadow

You can access this option either from the toolbar or the Format menu.

When you've finished, click anywhere on the page (outside the WordArt text) to return to normal Word operation:

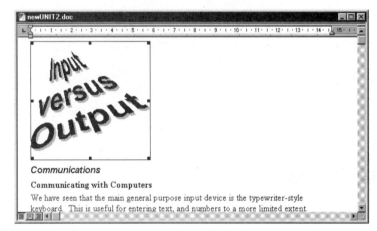

As with any embedded object, you can edit your WordArt at any time simply by double-clicking on it.

CHAPTER FOURTEEN

Tables and Charts

Tables allow you to organise and manage text in rows and columns. If a table contains numeric information, it is possible to depict this in chart form.

This chapter explores Word's range of table and chart features.

Covers

Creating A Table

1 Place the Insertion Point on a blank line in the document.

2 Click on the Table icon in the Toolbar, and drag downwards and to the right.

The further you drag, the larger the table. In this case a table of 4 rows and 3 columns is being created.

The table is inserted into your document:

HANDY TIP **You can resize a column by moving your mouse pointer to the border between the columns: it will turn into a black double headed arrow ←|→. You can resize rows in the same way.**

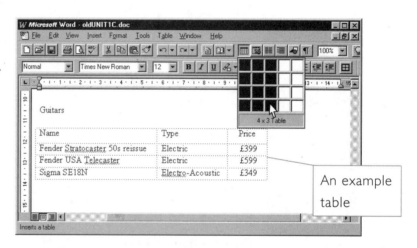

An example table

HANDY TIP **Hold down the Alt key to see the measurements in the ruler.**

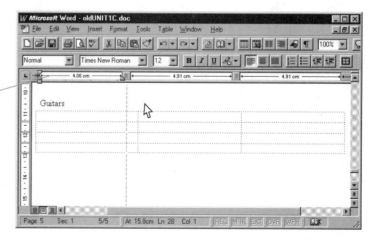

Entering Text

You can add text to your table by clicking in each cell in turn. All the normal formatting commands still apply.

A quick way to get to the next cell is to press Tab. Shift+Tab takes you back to the previous cell.

You can have more than one line within each cell. The Table row will expand to accommodate any extra text:

HANDY TIP

If you actually need to enter a Tab character, press Control+Tab

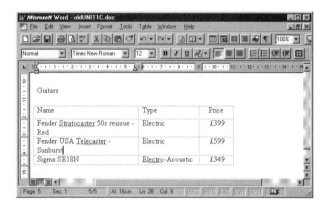

Formatting

You can format a whole row or column at once. To select a row drag across or click in the space just to its left.

REMEMBER

The same applies to columns. To select, click slightly above the top cell of the column.

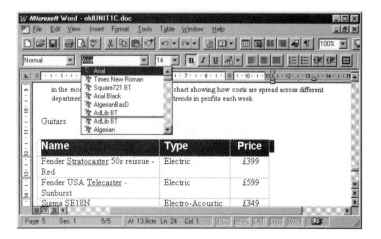

Inserting a Row/Column

1 Select the column to the right of where you'd like the new cells.

2 Holding down the right mouse button, choose "Insert Columns" from the pop-up menu.

The new column will appear to the left of the selected column.

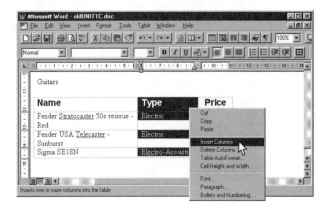

Cutting and Pasting

1 Select the row/column or cells.

2 Holding down the right mouse button, choose "Cut" from the pop-up menu.

3 Select the destination row/column or cells.

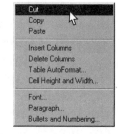

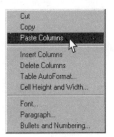

4 Hold down the right mouse button to access the "Paste" option.

The text is pasted back into the table, immediately to the left of the selected column.

Controlling Height and Width

To select an entire table, choose "Select Table" from the Table menu, or type Alt + Numeric keypad "5".

1 Select the cell(s) to change.

2 Choose "Cell Height and Width" from the Table menu.

3 Click on the Row tab, then the Column tab to see all the options available.

"Auto" sizes rows/columns according to the text inside.

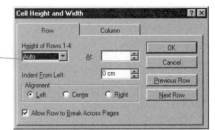

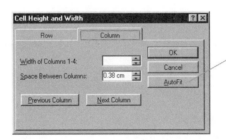

The AutoFit button proportions the column widths on the basis of the table size and the contents of the columns.

Merging Cells

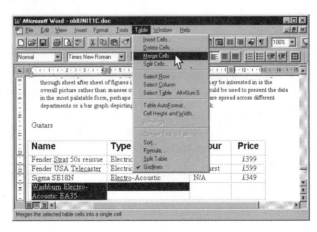

1 Select the adjacent cells to be merged.

2 Choose "Merge Cells" from the Table menu.

...contd

The cells have now been merged into one:

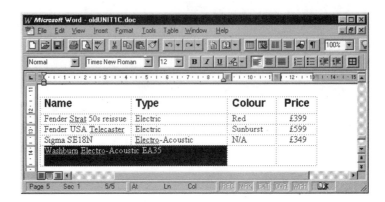

Formulae

In this example a column of figures has to be added up.

1 Click in the cell which is the destination for the calculation.

2 Choose "Formula" from the Table menu.

BEWARE

For the Sum function to work properly, all rows above the current cell must have the same number of columns. If you merged the cells for the last example, you will need to split them again (Table menu).

3 Enter the formula or select from the list of "Paste functions".

4 Choose the Number format and click "OK".

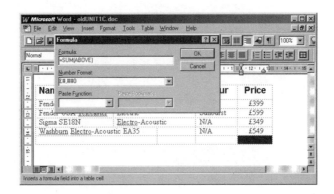

...contd

The result is added as a field, which may be recalculated if the numbers above change:

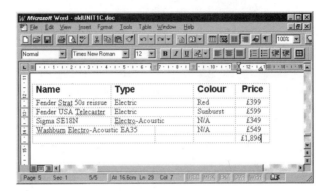

Borders and Shading

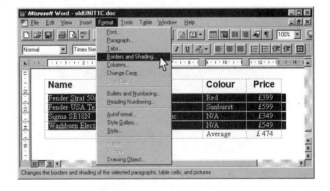

Select either the entire table or just a range of cells.

Choose "Borders and Shading" from the Format menu.

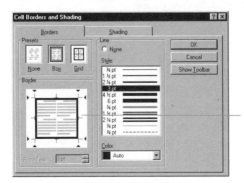

3 If necessary activate the Borders tab, and choose your borders options.

You can click on various parts of this diagram to activate different perimeter and internal lines.

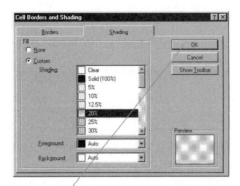

4 Now click on the Shading tab and set your shading preferences.

5 Click "OK". Your selected cells now have a border and shading applied.

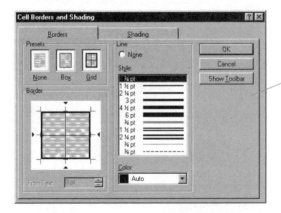

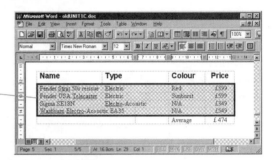

In this example the Borders dialog box has been used to set up a style for the lines *inside* the selected area.

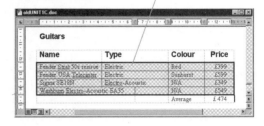

The Borders Toolbar

You can activate the Borders toolbar either from the View menu ("Toolbars" command) or by holding down the right mouse button on one of the existing toolbars.

Select the cell(s) to be formatted.

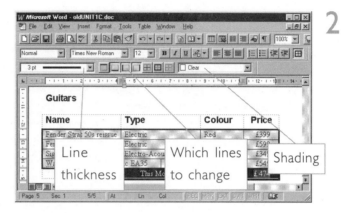

2 Select a line style then click on the appropriate line icon.

Line thickness

Which lines to change

Shading

Changing Shading

Select the cell(s) to change.

2 Choose a fill option from the pop-up menu in the toolbar.

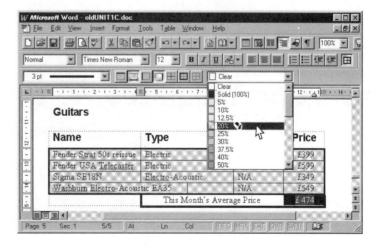

Using Borders on Ordinary Text

Note you can set borders and shading on any paragraph:

1 Select a normal paragraph of text.

2 Choose "Borders and Shading" from the Format menu.

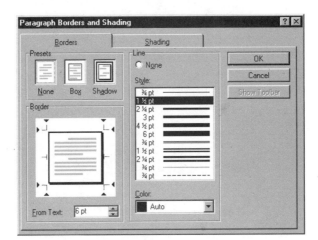

3 Select the desired border and shading features from the appropriate tabs.

Notice that the options in this dialog box are slightly different depending upon whether the selection is a table or ordinary text.

> Please allow 21 days for delivery. Prices and conditions are subject to change without notice.

Converting Tabulated Text into a Table

1 Select the tabulated text.

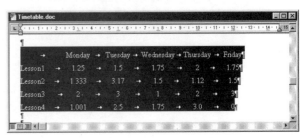

2 Choose "Convert Text to Table" from the Table menu.

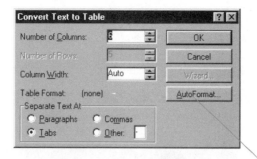

If you clicked "OK" at this point, the table would be set up with the correct number of rows and columns, but would still require manual formatting.

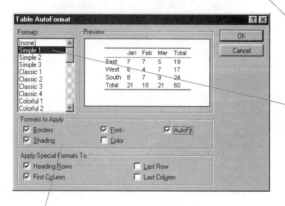

3 Click on the "AutoFormat" button.

4 Choose a table style from the "Formats" list, referring to the Preview box for guidance.

5 Select which aspects of formatting are to be applied.

6 Click "OK".

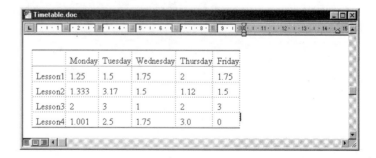

You can reverse this process with the "Convert Table to Text" command from the Table menu.

Creating a Chart from a Table

1 Select the data in the table.

2 Choose "Object" from the Insert Menu.

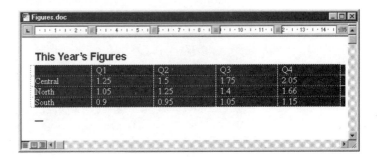

3 Choose "Microsoft Graph" from the Object dialog.

You can also activate the Chart application by clicking on the Chart tool: If this is not visible in Word 7, then right-click on a toolbar and choose "Customise". The Chart icon is available under the "Insert" category. From here you can drag it onto any toolbar.

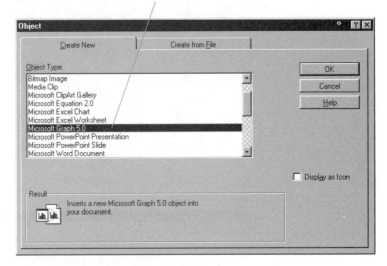

The Microsoft Graph mini-application is activated.

In Word 7 the Chart Wizard, which guides you through the Chart creation process, starts automatically.

In Word 6 you will see a default chart instead. You can then set the style options yourself using the "Gallery" menu.

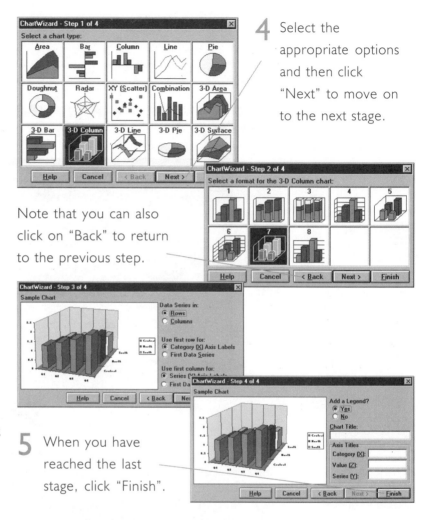

4 Select the appropriate options and then click "Next" to move on to the next stage.

Note that you can also click on "Back" to return to the previous step.

Microsoft Graph uses two main windows, one for the data and one for the chart itself. You can turn the datasheet on and off using the View menu, or the datasheet icon on the toolbar:

5 When you have reached the last stage, click "Finish".

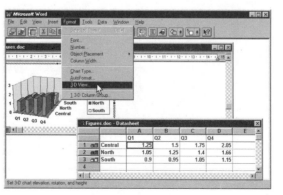

The chart is then generated, but can still be edited manually.

Formatting a Chart

1 From the format menu, choose "3D-View".

2 Enter the 3-D options and click "OK".

In this example we have changed the angle of rotation to 210 degrees, so it has completely turned around:

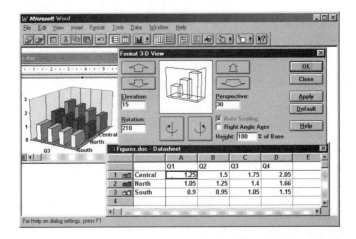

3 From the Insert menu, choose "Titles", check the Chart Title box and click OK.

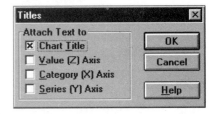

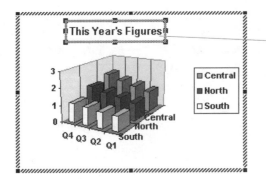

You can then manually edit the Title text:

...contd

You can customise the chart appearance simply by double-clicking on an element. For example, double-clicking on one of the bars will bring up a special formatting dialog:

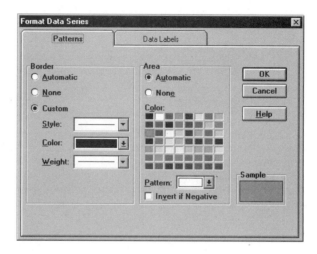

Importing Data

To bring in numeric data from an external source first click on the datasheet window, then choose the "Import data" command from the File menu.

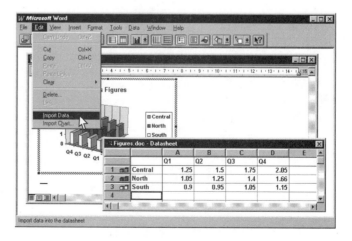

Number Format

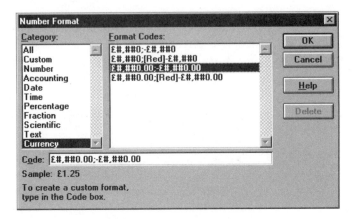

To access the number-formatting options:

1 Select some or all the cells in the Datasheet window.

2 Choose "Number" from the Format menu.

Returning To Word

REMEMBER

In Word 6 you can close down Microsoft Graph by choosing "Exit" from its File menu. Click "Yes" when asked to update the graph in the document.

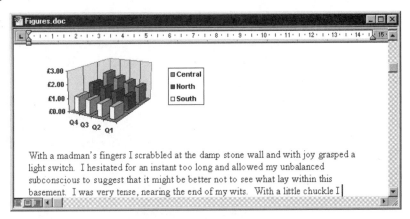

Clicking elsewhere in the document will return Word to normal operation.

Double-clicking on the chart will reactivate the Chart mini-application, allowing you to make further changes.

CHAPTER FIFTEEN

Sections

This chapter shows you how to break your document up into a series of sections. You can then apply different settings, such as multi-column displays, to individual sections as well as the complete document.

Covers

Defining Sections

1 Click an Insertion Point part of the way through your document (between paragraphs).

2 Choose "Break" from the Insert menu.

The Break dialog box appears.

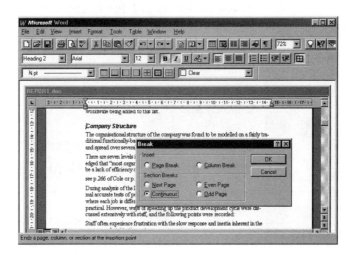

3 Choose the "Continuous" option, under Section Breaks.

4 Click "OK".

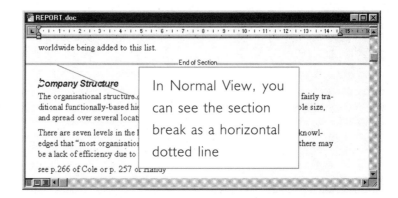

In Normal View, you can see the section break as a horizontal dotted line

The document is now divided into two sections.

Using Columns with Sections

1 Make sure you are using a document which has been divided into two sections.

2 Click an Insertion Point somewhere in the second section, then choose "Columns" from the Format menu:

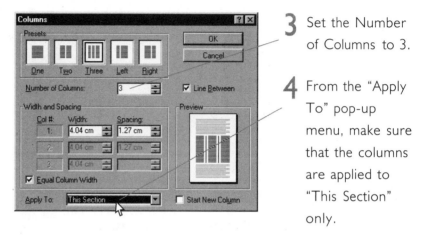

3 Set the Number of Columns to 3.

4 From the "Apply To" pop-up menu, make sure that the columns are applied to "This Section" only.

5 Click "OK".

You now have a mixed column layout:

HANDY TIP

If you drag with the Alt key held down, Word will display the horizontal measurements in the ruler.

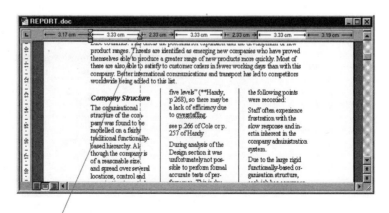

6 You can also adjust the width of columns by dragging the columns markers in the ruler.

Column Breaks

You can force text to start in a new column by inserting a hard break.

Place your Insertion Point and choose "Break" from the Insert menu.

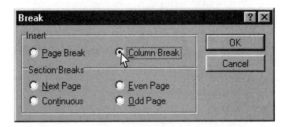

This will force the text after the Insertion Point into a new column.

Balancing Columns

1 Click an Insertion Point about two thirds of the way down the last column and choose "Break" from the Insert menu.

2 Insert a "Continuous" section break.

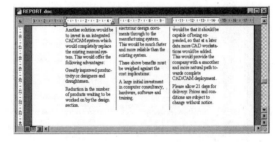

The columns are balanced to within one line of each other.

In this example there is also a page break after the three-column section.

Index